# BEYOND ANXIETY

# Beyond Anxiety

## THE CHRISTIAN ANSWER

### TO

| | |
|---|---|
| *FEAR* | *FRUSTRATION* |
| *GUILT* | *INDECISION* |
| *INHIBITION* | *LONELINESS* |
| | *DESPAIR* |

---

BY JAMES A. PIKE

---

*1953*

---

CHARLES SCRIBNER'S SONS

*NEW YORK    LONDON*

TO ESTHER

# ACKNOWLEDGMENTS

A DOCTOR'S PATIENTS may owe much to him; but he owes much to them: from his experience with them has come much of his understanding of illness and its cure. The same is true of the priest-counselor. Hence my first words of acknowledgment in connection with this book should go to the many individuals over the years who have taken up their problems with me, especially those who have reported their healing as well as their distress. Some of these may recognize themselves in these pages and thus know how they have contributed to my understanding; but I believe that I have been careful enough in dissimulation that they will not be recognized by others.

Then as to the matrices applied to the data (both in pastoral counseling and in this book) I owe virtually all that may be sound to a series of teachers and colleagues whose approach to theology has made evident the relevance of the Christian Faith to the real problems of human existence. Fortunately, I have been so situated that I have been able to continue in conversation with most of them over the years and can count them as personal friends. To name a few (but with no implication that any of them will be particularly pleased with these pages): The Rev. Howard A. Johnson of St. Augustine's College, Canterbury; the Rev. Prof. Charles W. F. Smith, of the Episcopal Theological School; the Rev. Canon Theodore O. Wedel, Warden of the College of Preachers, Washington Cathedral; the Rev. Prof. Albert T. Mollegen and the Very Rev. Stanley Brown-Serman, former dean of the Virginia Theological Seminary; the Very Rev. Hughell T. Fosbroke, former dean of the General Theological Seminary; the Rev. Prof. W. Norman Pittenger of the same Seminary, with whom I was privileged to serve as co-author of

*The Faith of the Church;* the Rev. Professors Reinhold Niebuhr, Paul Tillich, David E. Roberts and Cyril C. Richardson of the Union Theological Seminary.

My companion in the assimilation of what these men have had to say, in my reading and thinking, and in some of my pastoral work, and a constant encouragement in the writing of this book has been my wife, to whom its pages are dedicated. I am grateful also to Mr. William L. Savage, of Scribners, who four years ago encouraged me to undertake the work. Credit for much more than typing should go to Miss Virginia E. Rochelle, my secretary while it was being written: she checked the references, traced down quotations and made a number of constructive suggestions as to the substance. For the accurate and patient typing of revised drafts I am indebted to Mrs. Catherine M. Morton (and also to Miss Jean L. Joachim); for the reading of the proofs, to the Rev. Dr. William Turner Levy of the English Department of the College of the City of New York; and to Miss Dorothea Touraine who assisted with the index.

I hope that the benefit to the readers of this book may justify in a measure the contributions of so many. This much I do know: the problems here discussed are real ones—I have experienced most of them; and the answers are real (however inadequately I may have expressed them), for they have been my salvation.

JAMES A. PIKE

*The Deanery*
*New York City*
*August, 1953*

# CONTENTS

# CHAPTER I

# *ANXIETY AND BEYOND*

IT IS TO W. H. Auden that we owe the characterization of our time as the Age of Anxiety. Thoughtful people generally would agree with the designation, however much their views might differ as to the causes and cures.

Of course, this does not imply that men were not anxious before these days. But it seems that a great many more people—at least among the articulate, perhaps especially among the articulate—feel insecure. Further, large corporate factors, which are particularly marked in our age, have been operating as important causes for widespread uneasiness. These would include everything from the increased mobility of the population to our more widespread and devastating practice of war. For example, the very existence of nuclear physics throws a large parenthesis around all our little securities and puts a large $\pm$ sign in front, modifying all the little securities with a larger insecurity. If more people are more fearful, it is because there is more to be afraid of; if more people feel guilty, it is because they have more to be guilty about; if more people are plagued by a sense of meaninglessness, it is because there are fewer meanings left unthreatened. If these larger matters are part of the cause of the present malaise in personal life, then part of the cure is remedying these large disorders. Until we do no one will feel really secure. Thus no approach to personal security should proceed on the hope— or wish—that the individual can be rendered insensitive to

1

the kind of world he is in. We need to recognize in the realm of the spirit what for some time now we have recognized in the realm of the flesh: those interested in private health cannot afford to ignore public health. So it should be conceded at the outset that, since we live in a highly infected and infectious world, no man will be totally healthy, no matter what the personal situation of his life.

Yet those in the best position to lead us toward remedying our social ills of all sorts will obviously be those who have a good measure of personal security. Adolf Hitler is not so long dead as to allow us to forget where a neurotic can lead a nation—and the world; and all around us in recent decades we have been able to see that political tyranny and the voluntary relinquishment of personal liberty can follow from mass personal insecurity. So whatever our concern for the state of the world, it is important even for our social concerns that we turn our attention to insecurity as it affects the individual. And if we value each individual's life as significant, we should do this in any case. For while it is true that a bad social situation has a negative effect upon personal security, it is likewise true that a good social situation does not guarantee personal security. Often those with the least reason for external insecurity are in fact the most anxious. A man may think that if he simply had enough income his problems would be solved; but there are many people with adequate incomes who do not prove this up. A young lady may think that if she had a husband life would be fine; but there are many wives whose lives are not fine.

Therefore, fully cognizant of the bearing of the general situation of our times on personal security, and recognizing the importance of social concern and social action—especially on the part of healthy-minded individuals—we will focus our attention in these pages on what the author has found in his personal and pastoral experience to be the principal types of human anxiety. They are *fear, guilt,*

*inhibition, frustration, indecision, loneliness,* and *despair.*
One of the characteristics of our culture—and one which,
incidentally, has some bearing on these very difficulties—
is our great respect for the new and for the specialized.
Thus we tend immediately to assume that these are problems for the psychologists or—in their several ramifications—
for the psychiatrist, for the psychoanalyst, for the psycho-
therapist, or for the physician who is a specialist in psychosomatic medicine. This reaction certainly states a part
of the truth. Modern psychology, especially depth psychology and related disciplines, has indeed thrown a great
deal of light on the problems of human personality. The
introduction of the concept of the unconscious mind allows
us to see these problems "in depth" in a way never afforded
us, on the one hand, by the simple psychology of the conscious mind or, on the other, by "common sense." And, as
for older concepts which are still valuable, a better vocabulary has been provided for expressing them.

But it is no reflection upon the validity of a science or
on the contribution of its practitioners to emphasize its
limits in dealing with the human situation. A psychoanalyst,
for example, can provide, after hours of careful work, a
pretty good description of the forces at work in the unconscious and conscious levels of the patient's mind. From this
and from the patient's "history" he can form a diagnosis,
explain to the patient his condition more or less precisely,
and thereby lay the foundation for the therapy of self-
understanding. But any *cure* is going to come from the
imposition upon the data of a frame of meaning and a
scale of values, and from the introduction of spiritual resources. These frames of meaning, these value scales and
these resources—whether sound or unsound, whether helpful
or unhelpful—are *religious* rather than *scientific.*

Now to say that something is religious is not to say that
it is true, or to say that it recognizes the supernatural.

Here we use "religious" in the sense of *a view of life taken on faith,* that is, the ultimate premises by which one lives. To put it in minimal terms, any judgment about what is good or desirable as ends of life, as objectives of behavior, is a value judgment—a judgment based, in the nature of the case, not on scientific data, but upon one's religious perspective. For example, if an analyst finds that a patient is suffering from a sense of guilt and unravels the matter to show precisely what it is in the past that is creating this sense, the question is still open as to whether the patient was in fact guilty in the circumstances or whether the patient's attitude was a mere "complex." Should the analyst tell the patient that he was not guilty, he does not do this as psychologist; he does it as moralist. There is nothing "scientific" about the conclusion that there is no ground for guilt in given conduct, or about the conclusion that there *is* ground for guilt in given conduct.

The same distinction holds as to the *resources* for healing. When the psychologist enables the patient to understand himself better, this opens the way for bringing to bear upon the real situation in the patient's life whatever spiritual resources the convictions of the patient can make available; self-understanding does not in itself provide the right prescription for healing. Once the "is" is understood, judgments about "ought" are now no longer in the scientific field, but in the realm of belief. And here it is evident—popular assumption to the contrary—that it *does* make a difference what a man believes. Granted a proper diagnosis, whether a patient can be cured will now depend upon the resources available from his basic world view; it will depend on what kind of world he thinks it is, what he believes really matters in it, what he thinks his proper place is in it, and what sources of grace and strength he relies upon.

Of course, broad clinical experience can reveal what kinds of answers, if believed in, provide more healing and integration for the individual. In other words, clinical experience can tell us what answers, if true, would make sense in terms of the real problems of people. This, in turn, may make faith in certain answers more plausible than faith in others. But psychology does not itself supply the answers.

It is the thesis of this book that the Christian Faith supplies answers to the most basic questions which disturb the human spirit. Jesus said, "I am come that men might have life, and that they might have it more abundantly." If the Christian Faith is true, then a different face is put on the whole human situation. Man's problems will be set in a different context, since man's meaning and destiny will be different. The ground of man's security will be different. Into the picture will come resources for handling guilt and frustration which have no place in a secular and humanist world view.

But the application of the Christian Faith to the immediate problems of man's existence is by no means always obvious. That a connection may be made between the real problems and the true answers, two things are requisite. First, we must try to understand the real nature of human problems, and here we need all the light that can be thrown on the matter by psychology, logic, counseling experience, and common sense. Second, we must restate the relevant portions of the Christian Faith in terms which tie in with the problems that are defined. It is not that the knowledge of, for example, modern psychology has changed the Faith. The Christian Faith has outlasted the speculations of the philosophers and scientists of many an age. But new knowledge about the nature of the human mind and personality can help us state the Faith more relevantly and enable people to make more direct application of it to their genuine problems. Throughout the history of Christianity, and especially during its most creative periods, the Christian Faith has been translated and re-translated not only into different languages, but into different sets of concepts.

The fact that many people today are thinking about life in terms of the concepts of depth psychology (even the untutored read about these things in drug-store editions) is sufficient reason for our re-thinking the Christian Faith in these terms. However, there is an additional reason. The focusing of Christian thought in terms of explicit needs of human personality which transcend intellectual or ethical concerns in fact tends to restore the freshness of the Biblical approach to religion. The Biblical writers are, by and large, short on concepts, long on concern as to the human situation. The early Church carried this tradition forward: the articles of the Creeds are not just intellectual speculations. They are affirmations wrought out in the fire of personal and corporate experience and found to be abiding answers to perennial questions which affect the nature and direction of human life under God. (We shall see more fully in the pages which follow how this is so.)

In our concern to make the truth of the Judaeo-Christian heritage as relevant as possible to recognized psychological needs, we should at the outset recognize two real dangers. First, it is important that we view the task as one of translation, not of transference; that is, in our eagerness for contemporaneity, it is important that we not lose the Faith itself, that we not transfer our loyalties to hidden secularist presuppositions which often come wrapped up in the same package with psychological truth. Perhaps enough has been said above to suggest the proper distinction here.

The second danger is even more subtle. In their genuine eagerness to help people, preachers and counselors often hold forth God as a means to an end, rather than as the end itself. In short, God becomes a tool for man's advantage. Religion becomes a "resource" for personal fulfillment. Religion becomes a way to sleep better, or "to make friends and influence people." This, of course, is to make man God, and is ultimately irreligious. It turns prayer into "my will be done, with Thy help" rather than "Thy will be done, with my help." God is not something to be *used*. He is One to be adored and served. He is the end, not we. When a man has a right relationship with God, then he is saved; that is, he is whole. But it is irreligious to seek religion *in order to* become whole and healthy. "Seek ye first the kingdom of God and His righteousness," says Our Lord, "*and* all these things shall be added unto you." He did not say, ". . . *in order that* these things may be added unto you."

Now a recognition of our lacks and deficiencies without God and without a living faith can awaken us to our true religious needs; but true religion is a yielding up of our hopes and concerns to God as the end of our existence. A recognition of our inadequacies in personal fulfillment may well lead us to a complete reorientation, a redirection of our lives, a reordering of our value-structures. And hence it is right that we should give clear and thoughtful attention, in the light of knowledge from any source, to the sickness of our times and the anxiety of the individual. But just as it is wrong to say that we had better back up the Church *in order that* we may block communism, so it is wrong to say we'd better get religion in order to help cure our anxieties. If we are truly religious, we will be for God because He is God *and* his convictions will help to provide us with a stronger free society on the one hand and better personal integration on the other.

The concern that men be well, that they be freed from destructive forces in society and in personal life is certainly God's concern. And to help fulfill His will in this regard for ourselves and for our fellows we need all possible resources, not only the soundest insights of faith translated into the most relevant terms, but also all, by the way of analysis of man's condition and therapy for cure of the same, which can be afforded by psychology and by medicine. This principle applies not only to the breadth of general inquiry, but also to the means to be taken to help any given individual. The physician and the psychoanalyst can be ministers of grace in the healing of the whole man, not only in what they do as physicians and as analysts, but also by whatever sound religious and ethical understanding they can bring to bear on any situation by way of interpretation and cure. And for the many (presumably the majority) who do not need physical and psychical therapy, an analysis of their problems from the direction of religion and the focusing of the resources of religion upon them will be all the more effective if the spokesmen for religion take into account the insights and vocabulary of the medical and psychological sciences. Our respect for all of the avenues of understanding and of healing rests ultimately on the premise that all truth is God's truth, all healing is God's healing.

# Chapter II

## FEAR

FEAR CAN BE a good thing. It is a good thing to be afraid of the fearful. This is true in the simplest life-situations and in the most complex relationships. Fire is a fact and that it burns is a fact. So we hope our children will be afraid to put their hands in a fire. Similarly, there are certain objective factors involved in the soundness of a security. Fear as to the stocks in which you are now heavily invested, which leads you to investigate alternative possibilities and purchase sounder securities, is a good thing.

This kind of fear we most certainly do not want to get rid of. Since words are cheap and clichés are easier to provide than thoughtful analyses, in such fears we shall never lack the reassurances of acquaintances that "Everything will turn out all right." They tell us "I wouldn't give it a thought," or "You have nothing to be afraid of," when perhaps the very bottom is ready to drop out in some significant aspect of life.

Even gentlemen of the cloth, "popular" preachers, have been known to surround such platitudes with the odor of sanctity, with the aim of rooting out fears in a way that in fact is an opiate helping us to retreat from reality.

The first question we should ask ourselves when we feel afraid is: precisely of what am I afraid? The second question should be: what insecure elements are there in fact in the situation? And third: what, realistically speaking, can be done about it—either to change the situation or to shore it up?

Fear on this level, consciously faced and dealt with, can cause us no harm. The fear that harms us, that tears us apart, is more complicated—one that involves both levels of our mind, the conscious and the unconscious, and puts them in conflict. Deep anxiety comes from having put our trust in something that is ultimately untrustworthy. It comes from living a life for something which ultimately will not sustain life. To put it another way, it comes from placing ultimate reliance on the conscious level, on ends which, on the unconscious level, we know may "let us down." As long as fear, even a fear of this type, is at the conscious level, it is manageable, it can be dealt with and the situation which gives rise to the fear can be dealt with. It is when there is *conflict between the conscious and unconscious levels as to the degree of trust in any object of life* that the tension is created which is the typical anxiety of our times.

The things in which we place our ultimate reliance are our *gods*. It is interesting that the Old Testament writers have very little discussion of atheism. What they are concerned about is idolatry. We often miss the point of this concern, because we customarily limit our concept of "idol" to images worshiped by primitive peoples. Some idols do take the form of images, just as statues, pictures, and stained glass are used in the Christian tradition. But always behind the image is some life-interest, some aim or objective which has grasped the worshiper. It is a focus which he regards as significant in life. Worship can be defined as "worth-ship," giving worth to. Thus in the culture of the Baal-worshipers, fertility was the principal concern of life. And the liturgical practices (which we would call pornographic) associated with the cult are, in fact, relevant to a life-pattern in which the reproduction of animals and crops is paramount. Usually the ends which the idols represent are themselves good. Fertility is indeed of value.

But there are two things wrong with making such an end the ultimate basis of reliance (which is what worship is). First, fertility and growth do not cover all of the significant possibilities of life; and second, this basis of things is not ultimately reliable. In short, the idols are only partial in their "coverage" and they have feet of clay.

Let us see how this works out in a more modern example. If a man makes his business the end-all and be-all of his life, subordinating all else to it—family, ethical principle, even joy and pleasure—he is, in the sense we have been discussing it, an "idolater." As long as things go well he may be capable of a very high degree of integration, that is, of unification of personality around this one aim to which all else is subordinated in a pattern of behavior more or less reliable. But the same two difficulties are here, however; first, it results in a narrowing in the scope of the personality, indeed a transformation of the personality (we become like the gods we worship; if we worship brass, we become brass). And, second, when the idol of business success shows its feet of clay, the worshiper is let down, and sometimes goes so far as to die with his god (we need only to recall those who in November, 1929, jumped out the window as their gods died).

There are many people in such a situation of idolatry, that is, for whom something unworthy of such a place is given absolutely first place. For some it is business. For others it is social station: there are women who will sacrifice everything, even the family security, to this god. It may be sheer pleasure, in the maw of which is thrown possible career, the respect of others, duty to family. It may be a person. If it is the latter, even if the relationship is the most legitimate one, a person makes a poor god. When another person is made the ultimate end of life, life and personality are narrowed; and what is more, persons may "let us down"—and there is no person of whom this is not true. Many a parent has lived out his old age in bitter disillusionment because he made as the primary focus of life a child who on coming into manhood disappointed, or perhaps even rejected, the parent.

But long before the feet of clay actually show themselves, we often sense the insecurity of our situation when we have "put all our eggs in one basket" and we move on into a more complicated form of idolatry called polytheism.

Several years ago in a large Eastern city, a successful businessman in midlife began to show serious signs of anxiety, with a consequent effect on his health. His physician referred him to a psychoanalyst who readily sensed that a great deal of the man's difficulty came from the fact that over the years he had focused his attention almost entirely on his business, leaving little or no time for other aspects of life, and particularly for recreation. (This is an illustration of how an idol does not cover the whole of life.) The analyst suggested that he needed a mistress. "But," the patient explained, "I love my wife and have always been faithful to her." The analyst insisted that he needed a "new start" in his emotional life in order successfully to shift his interest from what had been the one focus. At length the businessman agreed and a convenient arrangement was worked out.

For a stretch he did feel a good deal better. He found that he really could enjoy life. But he began to be filled with regret that he had not enjoyed life in the years that had gone by. His regret began to take the form of the recognition that his wife, who had been the companion of his youthful labors and who had suffered through the days of privation (he was a "self-made man") had never had the opportunity to "enjoy life" as he was now enjoying it. As a result of this growing sense of guilt, he began to pay a great deal more attention to his wife. He began to "take her out" and shower affection on her. The attention to the two women was beginning to take a good deal of time from his business and this was especially serious since over the years he had developed his organization as a kind of "one-man show," never letting go of the reins enough to develop responsible leadership in others in the firm. But his concern for (though not his zest for) his business even increased because his need for money was a good deal greater now that he was "enjoying life" with two companions. Meanwhile he had developed a real affection for the young lady, and this was paralleled by a revived devotion to his wife—who was now reflecting his interest in a greater attractiveness. He had moved from a simple idolatry (which is called monolatry) to polytheism. Because one god did not cover the field, did not "fill the bill," he now had three gods, with no higher deity resolving the conflict among them. He did the only thing he knew to do—and this is a true story—he shot himself. *Polytheism in worship leads to schizophrenia* (split-personality) *in life.*

Whether a false centering of life takes the form of monolatry or polytheism, the result is anxiety. If one idol holds the field and all else is subordinated to it we will sooner or later begin to fear that this objective is not worth while, is not reliable. If we seek to meet this situation by setting up other idols for other realms of life, the conflicts between the idols become conflicts within ourselves. We become "split" personalities.

From this analysis we can see what the way to avoid fear and anxiety is. We need a single ultimate for our lives which meets four specifications: (1) it must be genuinely worth while; (2) it must cover the whole of life; (3) it must be something to which all other ends can be subordinated; and (4) it must be utterly reliable. With life integrated around such an end there will be no anxiety, no unhealthy fear.

Obviously, only God meets these specifications. It is He that is finally worth while. It is He that covers the whole field. To Him can all things be safely subordinated, without the loss of any of their positive values. It is He alone that is utterly reliable.

It is because all of this is implied in the very meaning of the word "God" that, for the Christian, God is *one*. Only one ultimate is needed. Any more ultimates would split up life. In short, the Christian answer to the problem of fear is the simple creedal affirmation I *believe in one God.* We do not mean "I believe that there is a God," but rather I believe *in*—that is, put my trust in—one God. A man who really does worship the one God will himself be really one.

This one God—this reliable answer to the problem of fear is well described in the familiar psalm: "In his hand are all the corners of the earth"—He covers the whole of reality, there is no place we can go where He isn't, no aspect of life to which He is not relevant; "a great King above all gods"—devotion to Him is capable of subordinating and ordering all other interests; "Let us heartily rejoice in the strength of our salvation"—He is utterly reliable; "We are the people of his pasture and the sheep of his hand"— He is personally concerned about us; He will not let us down.

A man had gotten behind in his debts; his bills were piling up. He began to get "second notices" from department stores and phone calls from some of his other creditors. He found it difficult to decide between the claims upon him; so he conferred with the manager of the local bank. The banker's advice was direct and simple: "Borrow from us what you need to pay all your bills; and then you'll have only *us* to worry about." This is a parable of the Christian answer to fear. If we really fear God, we need fear nothing else.

It is a false sentimentality that has set in opposition the

fear and love of God. If we trust in God, if we are grateful for the fact that we have Him to trust in, then inevitably we fear God. That is to say, we know Him as the only ground of our security and we fear lest we be distracted to other ends and lose our footing. If we love Him, we will fear lest we let Him down—Him Who does not let us down.

But we can't love or fear God if we don't believe in Him. How can we have faith?

This question is asked by two different kinds of people. There are those who really don't want to believe in God, who would be quite upset if something were to compel their belief in Him. Perhaps they have had a bitter and disillusioning experience with the Church and a belief in God might force them to re-examine a hatred that has become a treasured part of their personalities. Perhaps their way of life would be threatened. (A college student told a chaplain that he had lost his faith two years before. The chaplain wisely explored one possible cause by asking, "Think back: what significant change in your conduct took place two years ago?") Sometimes unbelievers have been so cocksure in airing their views that pride makes them rather protective of their unbelief. Sometimes a complex unconscious pattern impels the rejection of all authority: deepseated hostilities can ascend even to the Most High.

But there are many people who really *want* to believe, who sense that if they could believe, their anxieties would be remedied, their lives would be richer and fuller—yet somehow they cannot.

While words alone cannot create faith, it is possible to remove some of the road-blocks which have been erected by common misconceptions about the nature of belief. The first of these is the idea that the existence of God is something to be proven. This idea rests on an unspoken assumption (shared by some who would call themselves believers) that God is to be conceived of as a being beside other beings, another thing in the universe alongside of the things we are sure of, and something to fit in with a set of notions we already hold. Actually if God is at all, He is the Ultimate Ground of all being, His existence is the great First Premise from which our view of life is to start, and belief in Him is the perspective from which we are to view the rest of reality. If we could prove Him up it would mean that we already stood on some firmer, more basic ground and from that vantage point reasoned up to Him. Then He wouldn't be God—He would be less ultimate, less basic than whatever we started our thinking with.

In any case we start with faith. Any geometry student knows that axioms precede theorems. For the true believer God is the Great Axiom; all his interpretations and evaluations of the various elements of reality take their start from there. This process is not unique to theism; it is true of the believer in anything. It is true of the materialist, that is, one who has decided that matter is the ultimate reality and that all else is derivative. This operating principle he accepts by faith; he has not proven it. The same is true of the humanist, who has decided to believe that man is the highest reality; he cannot *prove* that there is no higher reality.

If we believe in God it will not be because we have "proved" His existence but because assuming His existence makes more sense out of things than assuming His non-existence. And this is true of all the other elements of belief and of our acceptance of the Christian world-view as a whole. In a measure our conviction as to the greater plausibility of the Christian Faith (as over its alternatives) will come from our consideration of the universe as a whole. But it will come especially from an understanding of that part of the universe with which we are best acquainted and with which we are most concerned—our personal lives.

Here the test is: does the Christian Faith provide a better answer to crucial personal problems? By "better" we mean more healing answers, answers which better fulfill the personality, better relate people one to another. This question determines the method used in these pages as we take up one problem after another: an exploration of the real nature of each problem and then the application to it, as understood, of the resources of Christian belief and practice. If the light of the Christian Faith both provides the best understanding of the problems and offers the most salutary solution to them, we will have both a deeper and more realistic understanding of what the Faith is and a sounder reason for believing in it.

A second "road-block" to trust in God is the widespread notion that religious belief is not "scientific." It is not. Religious verities cannot be established by the "scientific method"; spirit will not be discerned in any test-tube. But to go further and imply that nothing exists which cannot be encompassed by the laboratory methods of natural science is not to be scientific; it is to import a dogma into the situation—this is "scientism," not science. And it is a dogma which, if consistently applied, would rule out many other things than religious realities—such as love, friendship, honor, duty, and poetry. It would even rule out basic unproven assumptions on which the scientist himself operates, such as the reality of any phenomena outside of his own mind, and the worth-whileness of truth.

Science can do something with the physical make-up of a rose, but it has no tools for explaining or evaluating the full truth about the rose, which includes its beauty. (Not even the test of symmetry is conclusive, because the asymmetrical things are sometimes the most beautiful.) Science can dissect a human body, but it cannot encompass the unique nature of a particular man or woman. The more personal and particular a phase of life is, the less competent is science to deal with it. The more a situation involves values, the less appropriate is the scientific method. Now, God is the ultimate Truth, the ultimate Value, the Ultimate Personality, and is the ultimately Unique One, and thus science is at its maximum of incompetency when it comes to dealing with Him. Belief in Him is neither scientific nor unscientific.

While belief in God is beyond proof and beyond science, the way to faith in fact parallels the steps in scientific proof. First comes the hypothesis. The scientist doesn't take every hypothesis into the laboratory; he will not waste time and materials trying out whatever comes into his head. He will select a hypothesis that, if true, would make sense out of the body of data with which he is concerned. Then he carefully tests the hypothesis in the laboratory. If the hypothesis fits the facts, then it is a truth; it joins the body of knowledge.

So with the way of faith. Life is too short to give sustained experiment to every view of reality. You should select that one which seems the most plausible, that is, that one which, if true, would seem to make the most sense out of the world around you and the world within you. You may well come to feel that the view of life most adequately taking account of all levels of reality is belief in God as made known to us in Jesus Christ. But you are still in the realm of hypothesis, not that of knowledge. The hypothesis should now be tested in the laboratory. But in the case of the Christian Faith, the laboratory must be your own life. Nothing else will do, because that Faith is primarily concerned with what can only so be experienced: God's relation to you, and your relations—under God— with other people. *You must live it* for hypothesis to turn into knowledge; for the testing to be a thorough-going one you must throw no less than yourself into the testing; you must "bet your life" on it. Then, as better order is made out of your life, as your fears give way to trust, as real joy replaces distress, as your relations with others are more fruitful and wholesome (for you and for them), as you understand your past better and your steps toward the future are more steady—then you *know*. "If any man will do His will, he shall know of the doctrine," said Jesus. After the leap of faith, what was hypothesis is now knowledge. Then we can, with the early Christians, witness to "that which was from the beginning, which we have heard, which we have seen with our eyes, which we have looked upon, and our hands have handled, of the Word of Life" (1 John 1).

The best way to have belief in God is to start living as though He exists, to rearrange one's objectives and aspirations as though His promises were true, praying all the while, "Lord, I believe, help Thou my unbelief." To such a plea the idols are silent. In this crisis, as in others, the idols let us down. The true God will answer by fire.

# Chapter III

# GUILT: 1

If God is, then we have a dimension for understanding the "guilt complex." Sometimes it's just guilt. Guilt can be defined as the gap between the *ought* and the *is*. And this gap causes us trouble. It is a gap that has to be closed in one way or another. And as we shall see shortly, one way of trying to close it is to call it a "complex."

Why can't we manage a feeling of guilt? Because it is altogether necessary that a man accept himself. A man can't hold his head up, can't face his world or keep on his job, can't be whole, unless he can think he's all right, that he is acceptable. *Self-acceptance* is a basic element in personal security and effectiveness. This is why we make such strenuous efforts at rationalization, why we so seek to put ourselves in the right.

These rationalizations take many forms. The easiest "blanket" treatment is to lower the law for life and thus eliminate or reduce the gap between the "ought" and the "is." For many in American life the modern version of the Pharisee's speech in the temple (though perhaps made in the locker room) would be: "I mend my fences, pay my taxes, don't kick my neighbor's dog. I don't talk religion or butt into other people's business." Or maybe there is added: "I'm a good Rotarian" or "a good Elk." Such a standard is hardly the Golden Rule, which often the same people say is the only thing that matters. But sometimes anything so brittle as a rule named after a metal is replaced by a rubber rule—the conduct of one's acquaintances: "I'm as good as the next fellow" (though perhaps such a one is the first to jump on said next fellow, should he step on his toes). This is one reason many "rejoice in iniquity" or (as a modern translation of St. Paul puts it) "delight in statistics of evil" à la Kinsey; it makes the "next fellow" norm even more tolerable. Or in a similar vein, we sometimes admit fault in such a way as to dismiss it: "Sure, I have my faults; who doesn't?"—implying that nothing can be, or need be, done about the fact. Some go all the way and reduce the norm to the *exact* measure of their own moral stature: "That's just the way I am," sometimes adding an item or two in a bill of particulars, e.g., "I've *always* had a bad temper: I can't help it."

Sometimes we look to external circumstances to relieve ourselves of responsibility: "I was a dead-end kid" or "I couldn't take it any longer." Sometimes we relieve ourselves by focusing on some supposed good that has come out of what would otherwise seem evil: "I really told her off; but it'll do her a world of good!" (to do her a world of good being, of course, the reason for telling her off!).

In these latter days such rationalizations have for many attained to sophistication through the efforts of prevalent brands of psychology—especially in the popular handbook presentation. The question-begging labeling of all guilt as "complex," the overemphasis on family influences by the Freudians and of social conditioning by certain sociologists, the sheer relativism in morals preached by popular anthropologists—all give dignified sanction to eliminating the gap between the "ought" and the "is," and have given moderns "self-acceptance" on what appears to be bargain-counter terms—but actually as we shall see shortly, at a heavy price in terms of abiding inner security. In any event, all of this, whether on the level of lay cliché or of professional jargon, is a recognition of what a desideratum self-acceptance is.

But there is an equally essential trait: *self-criticism*. If a person lacks self-acceptance, he can't live with himself; if he lacks self-criticism, others can't live with him. To have real self-criticism there must be a norm. If a man is his own measure, or if his contemporaries are his measure, the fruitful tension is gone out of life; or, to change the figure, nothing has any real purchase on life. For Christians there is a norm which not only brings the best man under judgment, but also brings under judgment the "best standards" of any given culture.

> Thou shalt love the Lord thy God with all thy heart, and with all thy soul, and with all thy mind. This is the first and great commandment. And the second is like unto it; Thou shalt love thy neighbor as thyself. On these two commandments hang all the Law and the Prophets.

In short, we are commanded to give our full time to God. Here are no easy rules which can be managed by a reasonable degree of decency or social conformity, leaving the bulk of our time and resources free to do as we wish. It means that our every action, word and thought are judged as to whether or not they further God's purposes in the world. No rule-book or code can embrace such a demand. At one time it may say, "You should have worked today instead of playing." Another time it may say, "You should have relaxed today rather than working." For one it may say, "You should stick to what you're doing, instead of wishing you were something else in life." To another it may say, "You should stop doing what you are doing (though in itself it's good and worth doing) and do something else which is a better use of your particular talents." Sometimes this law may say, "This person needs more of your time"; sometimes, "This person should have less of your time."

This "whole law" affords a deeper basis for conforming to the best in the mores. But it also tells us that the mores are never enough and indeed it sometimes means that keeping the mores is positively wrong.

This is what was wrong with the morality of the Pharisees in the familiar parable: "Jesus spake this parable unto certain which trusted in themselves that they were righteous." The Pharisee said, "I fast twice in the week, I give tithes of all that I possess." The trouble was not necessarily that he did these things. In general, they are good things to do. The question is, what about the rest of his time and means? Had he brought all of it under judgment he wouldn't have felt particularly superior to the publican. True, the latter was in a wrong calling (a tax-collector for the Romans, hence a collaborationist), but still in the course of a week it is likely that he, too, did a few things with his time that were in furtherance of God's purposes: a friendly act here, an expression of loyalty there (there is honor even among thieves!)—and who can judge the relative value of two persons' meagre part-time performance? Suffice it to say neither lived up to God's demand. And the publican was the better off, because he was conscious of the fact.

Consciousness of one's guilt is an essential condition to the process of self-acceptance which Christian faith offers. This is the meaning of Jesus' words: "Even the harlots shall enter the kingdom before ye righteous ones." The life of the prostitute is so obviously out of joint, so obviously is lacking in fulfillment, that it is difficult for her to feel acceptable on her own merits—unlike the respectable.

A good lawyer will not reach for the statute and case books until he has heard a statement of the facts. A good physician will not reach for his prescription blank until he has made a diagnosis; he cannot heal a wound until the wound is laid bare.

Here are some questions which may help some to make conscious the actual fact of guilt. We might label them "An Examination of Conscience for the Respectable."

What things really matter most to you in life? (A good test: what things are important enough to you to keep you lying awake at night?) Worked out in a priority scale, is God and His will really at the top? Are there things you want very much that you would feel uncomfortable praying for? Are there things that matter to you (though perhaps acceptable enough in themselves) which leave little or no room for things that ought to matter to you?

Those working for you: Do you treat them as persons, with real concerns and personal needs like your own, or as means to getting done what you want done? In other words, do you "use" them? Do you seek to find ways to bring out in them the best opportunities for expression and fulfillment, and the best chance for joy in their work?

Those for whom you work: Are you really concerned for the larger aims of which your piece of work is a part, or is your job primarily conceived of as a means to getting the things you want? In the assertion of your own demands do you take into account the situation and interests of your employers? In other words, do you treat them as persons? Are you honest in the full commitment of your time, and in giving your best energies while on the job? in assuming responsibility for your mistakes as readily as for your merits? Or do your defense-mechanisms get into operation at any point of criticism? Can you be "counted on"?

Those with whom you work: Are you concerned about the well-being of your colleagues? Do you really rejoice in their achievements, really regret their failures?—or rather vice versa! Are you as alert in sharing credit as you are in shifting blame? How concerned are you about the needs of their personalities—for example, whom are you apt to ask to go to lunch with you: someone whom you enjoy or who "builds you up," or some shy, unimportant soul to whom companionship and interest would mean much?

Those at home: What kind of atmosphere is created by your arrival at home in the evening, or in what mood do you greet those who arrive? Do you give out your best— in terms of positive interests that are shareable, or do you "dump" the worst of your moods and reactions on your family? By your warm interest in others do you nourish the fragile yearnings and possibilities striving for expression? What priority scale of values is likely to be formed in your children by your conversation? (The content of the dinner conversation is highly indicative and formative as to "what things matter.") Do you seek to provide each member with opportunities for real significance in the family life? Are you overly possessive towards your children?

Your acquaintances: Do you really enter into them seeking to know them on the deeper levels rather than on trivial bases? Do you encourage in them the best possibilities? Are they better people for knowing you? Are you concerned enough about their problems to give the same thoughtful analysis to them as you would to your own, or do you take the easy way out afforded by platitudes of the "It's-always-darkest-before-the-dawn" type? Do you help lull into a feeling of righteousness when you should be candid, in all charity; for example, when you say "What more could anyone expect?" or "You did absolutely right"?

Are you more alert to pass on gossip than to pass on good report? Do you go out of your way to pass on to others the praise you have heard about them (the most convincing and satisfying way for one to receive it)? Do you build others up when they need it (and when don't we need it?) or do you "belittle"? Have you let people down, not carrying through your commitments? Do you apologize when you have hurt others? Have you always made things right?

Where do you get your norms for forming your opinion on political and social issues? From the circles in which you move? From consideration of the best benefit to your business, class, race? Or do you use higher norms as a judgment on all current values, even those which seem to benefit you? Is your work in the community a positive influence against evil—evil that is legal no less than that which is illegal, that which is respectable no less than that which is disreputable? How often have you been willing to back up unpopular causes?

Then the more obvious things: Do you lose your temper? (Watch for rationalizations here.) Are you loyal to your spouse—in thought and intention no less than in body? Are you absolutely honest—in word as well as in act?

What about the way you use your money? (This, too, is under judgment, since it's not *your* money; all things are God's and we are to use them as His stewards.) How do you use your time? Is enough time saved for healthful recreation, for rest? Do you "dissipate" your energies in meaningless activities, stay up too late, eat or drink too much? (All this is God's business, because we are His and He wants us effective for His service.) Is enough time given to prayer and "getting your sights" spiritually, by good reading and meditation? Do you witness, by worship, to His presence and work in the world? (Watch rationalizations here.)

Do you share with others the spiritual roots which bear fruit in your life, or are you content merely to share some of the fruits from time to time? How many people have you helped come to a spiritual understanding of their own lives and problems, or put in touch with sound religion?

Anyone could add his own questions—and answers. "We have left undone those things we ought to have done;

and we have done those things which we ought not to have done."

Yet all of these questions do not reveal the full gravity of the situation. Each of us in reviewing his own biography sees looming up in memory grievous events which no general questions could cover, but which actually are of more significance than the matters easily covered by questions. A calculated course of conduct which deflected the course of another's whole life. Neglect of duty which really mattered to someone. Gross disloyalty, bred of plain selfishness, in the face of the simple trust of others. Things which are past, but their being past adding to their weight: situations nothing can be done to remedy, where the doors are closed. We can't "make up" for them; we can't "fix them up." Or, if years have gone by and our consciences compel an attempt to repair, for example, a broken personal relationship, how likely it is that the scene has so shifted, life has so moved on, that unreality defeats the most well-designed attempts; regret is magnified, and things are still at loose ends. Or it may well be that new responsibilities make it impossible, without wrong to present loyalties, to attempt to "make up" for past neglects.

Truly, "the remembrance of them is grievous unto us; the burden of them is intolerable." Not *was* but *is*. Thus, past things can drag us down in the present: they are carried as dead weight.

No wonder we seek to excuse and forget: we can't carry such a load. No wonder we seek to get rid of it. Now, if our rationalizations and defenses really succeeded in making us feel acceptable, they could perhaps be justified therapeutically, even though they fell short of strict honesty. But they do not succeed. *Rationalizations do not get rid of a sense of guilt;* they are literally a "cover up": they cover guilt up like blankets and it sinks into the unconscious. This may free our conscious mind. But the guilt is there and the sense of guilt is there. If covered up, in the unconscious it remains; it festers, and it makes us sick (not only in spirit, but in body as well, the psychosomatic experts tell us). And one thing is sure: time does not heal the wound. Time dulls the conscious memory, but the live character of these events in the unconscious is evident from the vivid nature of "flash-backs" in day-dreams, not to mention the almost photographic accuracy with which dreams portray aspects of events which have deeply seared us. A passage in a novel, a scene in a play or motion picture, a chance meeting, will bring back in full force things we thought had passed out of our lives. The unconscious can regurgitate, but it never digests.

And this affords a clue as to why many of us live as we do. The way we fill every waking moment with activity, with sense impressions from the present, especially with trivial ones. We must always be doing something, be talking or be talked at. Illustrative is the way a radio blares all day as a housewife goes about chores which would not of themselves sufficiently occupy the conscious mind; or the way the evening hours in many a family are given to gazing into a machine which will provide ballast for the consciousness to leave no room for the demons from below. And many turn to alcohol. More will be said about this a little later; but here it should be pointed out that it is a double-edged sword. It stimulates the sense of well-being; at the same time it relaxes the barrier between conscious and unconscious and helps release the demons who sometimes reign, especially the morning after.

The increase in leisure in our times increases in turn the problem of finding "distraction." This is the tragedy of so many vacations. Dog-tired from a hyper-active year, a man "lets down" in a place where the phone doesn't ring and to which most of his correspondence isn't forwarded. Its remoteness, the absence of social obligations, the lack of pressures seem at first like heaven itself. But as his mind gradually clears of current items and his body and mind have sufficiently relaxed—with "the pressure off," the trap-door from the unconscious opens more easily and a veritable floor-show of demons prances across his consciousness. Indeed, for the first time he sees the wrong of some things in the years that are past; he understands why a given relationship broke off; why there was resistance to a given plan; why he incurred the dislike of someone. Then the "cellar gang" makes its appearance: events he had mulled over before and "covered up" with rationalizations: they are laid bare in all their original unpleasantness, with condemning finger raised. And the statute of limitations never runs.

But out of the Pandora's Box comes more than guilt feelings. Inextricably mixed up with the images are resentments and hostilities, regrets that we didn't assert ourselves *more,* that we didn't "say our piece" or "tell them off." And then, paradoxically enough, as to some sins of sense, guilt is intertwined with desire, regret that one sinned at all alternating with regret as to failure to follow up some "opportunities" or wish that the past were present. And then, in turn, we are besieged by new regrets for these hostilities and lusts, and the estimate of ourselves sinks lower and lower.

Suggestive is the parable of the one and seven devils. Freed from the demon of "pressure" the conscious mind is "swept and garnished" and then seven worse devils occupy the place—and "the last state of that man is worse than the first." Thus the rush to fill up the house with more cheerful visages—the time in the vacation when a man says "I don't want just to sit around." Now there is the rushing hither and yon, the bustling activity, the burgeoning of cocktail parties, the place filled with acquaintances—or others. Then the "fidgetiness" to return to the office (which in this situation is *not* simply the healthy reaction to enough rest). And finally he returns, more exhausted and worn in body and spirit than upon his departure.

Of course, this narrative is a burlesque of what for many are relatively good vacations. But it is meant to underline real experiences in anyone's leisure time, these in turn pointing to what goes on in the unconscious *all the time*, whether or not at the given moment the demons are rearing their ugly heads.

So we cannot get rid of a sense of guilt by simply covering it up. Yet get rid of it we must if we are to accept ourselves. How can we?

# Chapter IV

## GUILT: 2

THE PROBLEM IS not unlike that of garbage-disposal. You can't leave it around the kitchen; nor can you lock it up in the cupboards and closets. You usually arrange to have some agency take it off your hands. So with guilt: we can't live with it, we can't afford to hide it in the unconscious (by denying that it is guilt); we need it taken off our hands.

*That God will lift our guilt from us is the good news of the Gospel.* At the heart of the universe are resources for absorbing the guilt of the world. God can take it; we can't take our own guilt, but He can.

This is why for Christians the Cross is the central symbol. In Christ, God is tipping His hand; we see how He always is, has been and will be. In Christ, God has translated Himself into the language of a human life, entered our estate, met us where we are. On the Cross we see Him "taking it," taking up the slack between His aweful righteousness and our sinfulness. We could not measure up to Him; so He comes down to us.

Christ Who was tempted even as are we, but Who knew no sin took on the hurt of all sin. In the Cross we see God reconciling His justice—the basis of our self-criticism, with His mercy—the basis of our self-acceptance. God at least indulges in no rationalizations: with Him sin is sin, wrong is wrong—and on this depends the stability of the moral universe. So He takes into Himself the burden of sin. That is a great secret of the universe, revealed in Christ. *God was in Christ reconciling the world unto Himself.*

For us, this means simply, we can accept ourselves. *We can accept ourselves because the ultimate Ground of the universe accepts us—though unacceptable.* Thus is preserved both self-criticism and self-acceptance—both absolutely essential to our well-being.

Hundreds of volumes have been written on the Doctrine of the Atonement, analyzing the *how* of God's saving action; yet when all is said and done this is a mystery. But the *fact* of the matter has been discovered by millions of Christians for themselves over twenty centuries. The power of the Cross is a fact, however explained. He said: *If I be lifted up, I will draw all men unto me.* And so it has been ever since. Men, tortured in conscience, have turned in confidence to Him, have been freed from the burden of guilt, and have gone on in peace and effectiveness. They have left behind them the debris of years. For them there has been granted the petition of the old prayer: "Though we be tied and bound with the chains of our sins, yet let the pitifulness of Thy great mercy loose us."

Yet pride is so much to the fore with us that few of us like to admit that we are "tied and bound with the chains of our sins." Surely we can extricate ourselves by the exercise of our wills; surely, then, we can live decently on our own power. Of this perennial hope (symbolized by the "New Year's Resolution") two things must be said: First, if we lived according to God's total law of love all our days from now on, still we are men with bad pasts, we are already "in the red" and we have no way of "making up" for our past sins. If an examination is set for which 70 per cent is passing, then it is possible to pass even after writing 50 per cent on the first question; after all, one *may* make 90 per cent on the second question. But if 100 per cent is passing, then a failure on the first question means a failure on the whole test. Now under God's law for life, 100 per cent is passing—"thy *whole* heart, thy *whole* soul, thy *whole* mind, thy *whole* strength." If, after a sinful yesterday, I do good all day today, well then today I have barely kept the law—I haven't earned any extra credits: Jesus said, "When ye have done all that ye are commanded to do, say, We are unprofitable servants."

But there is another sense in which we are "tied and bound with the chains of our sins." In our decisions as to particular matters of conduct, we are not as free as we tend to think. What we do in a given instance is not a simple matter of deciding to do good or deciding to do evil; in fact, in much that is the worst we do (for example, our spontaneous reactions to people and our social attitudes) we don't even go through the motions of weighing right and wrong. Essentially we *do* what we *are*. And what we are includes, as we have already seen, the makeup of our unconscious depths. In the unconscious is an assortment of urges, impulses, influences—some conceptual, some emotional; some constructive, some destructive; undigested guilt; half-buried hostilities; memories, fragmentary and whole; matrices molded by the society around us, impacts made upon us by family and by individuals. All these things play their part in what we do. So, sound depth psychology indeed is St. Paul's analysis: "The good that I would, I do not: but the evil which I would not, that I do. I find then a law, that, when I would do good, evil is present with me. For I delight in the law of God after the inward man: But I see another law in my members, warring against the law of my mind, and bringing me into captivity to the law of sin."

How, then, are we responsible for our wrongdoing? Are not the secular psychologists who accept determinism correct in writing off sin and guilt?

The fact that this "writing off" does not get rid of the

sense of guilt points to the fact that we do regard ourselves as responsible nevertheless, and this universal intuition is sound, because of a number of factors:

First, we have by past wrong choices furnished the unconscious with much that now weakens our ability to do right. An analogy from the field of criminal law: a man is culpable for injury to another from drunken driving, though in his condition he can't help it; he chose to drink what he drank.

Second, as to social patterns, we are part of society and are jointly responsible for the warpedness of the world around us: we are affected by its wrong, but our actions have contributed to it.

Third, as to influences of others, we are responsible for what company we have kept.

Finally, even for the most "irresponsible" acts, we blame ourselves—with sound intuition—for what we *are* that made us *do* what we did. To be more specific: we know that, in a given instance, we chose as we did because our values were wrong, our priority scale was badly set up. Light is thrown on this by an experience familiar to the counselor: A woman whose marriage is "on the rocks," tells you all the things wrong with her husband—for example, his chief interests are making money and spending it in drinking and gambling, his taste in companions is bad, he has never had any "spiritual" interests, and so on. So far she spares herself any of the blame. But a good question to ask at this point is: What was there about you that made you want to marry a man of this caliber? In short, what was your value-pattern? And right here is our realm of greatest freedom of spirit: *we can choose what we will value,* though all the influences—conscious and unconscious, personal and social—impinge here too. We know that we can transcend all such influences and choose what we will be *for* in life. Here we tie in to our discussion in Chapter II—this comes down to what our gods are; we are

free to choose what we will worship. In the last analysis
"religious freedom" is the only freedom.

The simplest solution to the whole business would, of
course, be to keep the law: to make the "is" of one's life con-
form to the "ought." This is so obviously desirable that many
people, even religious ones, have sought to reduce the
"ought" to a code which is relatively manageable. The
Pharisee was operating on this basis when he stood in the
temple and said: "I have prayed daily in the temple, fasted
twice in the week, given alms to the poor." Notice that Jesus
in telling the parable says that the Pharisee was here "seeking to *justify* himself": it was an attempt to meet the
problem of self-acceptance, except that, unlike many moderns, the Pharisee knew that the basis of his self-acceptance
was his acceptance by God. As we have already seen, what
was wrong with the Pharisee was not this concern, nor was it
wrong to have fasted, prayed, or given alms. These are good
things to do, and for that matter our Lord does not question
that he had in fact done them. What was wrong is that the
Pharisee thought that when he kept every jot and tittle of his
code—which was in fact the strictest of his times—that he
had done all that was required of him, and that he had earned
the right to acceptance. But Jesus' understanding of what
is expected of us, stated in the two great commandments,
means that when we have kept even the best set of rules we
have really just begun. Over and above any rules (and sometimes in contradiction to conventional rules) is the high demand of love for God and neighbor which calls for imaginative, on-the-spot positive ethical action in each particular
situation—action of a type that is so tailor-made to each life
situation that it is impossible to box it up in codes and rules.
In short, under the two great commandments we are to be on
the job for God twenty-four hours a day, utilizing all our
talents, and all our weaknesses, in the way that will best carry

out God's will for us as we see it. This does not mean we are all to be in the ministry, but it does mean that we are all to do whatever we do as a ministry. It does not mean we are never to relax and play, but it means that even our relaxation is done in the service of God, in terms of our greater usefulness to Him and in terms of His will that we enjoy with Him His creation. It does not mean that we empty our bank-accounts upon the appeal of the next "neighbor" who presents his need: a priority scale taking into account all the responsibilities that we have must enter the picture; but in giving or withholding we are to do it for God.

Now even this does not state the full measure of our responsibility under God: it certainly makes no sense to say that I am bound to try to meet the need of this particular homeless family and yet have no responsibility to seek to further low-cost multiple-unit housing that this family and many families like it may not be in such need. It would be quixotic indeed to say that I should help rehabilitate a particular youthful offender whom I happen to run into, but have no responsibility to work for the betterment of conditions in the slums from which he and many like him came. And so with my moral responsibility for the many social evils in the city of which I am a part, of the nation and of the world of which I am a part.

But with the "ought" put on this level—as a 100 per cent claim upon me—obviously I cannot "justify" myself. Suppose for one day I do live my life in perfect stewardship of my time and my energy. Then I have just barely kept the law; I have done nothing more with which to balance off my shortcomings of yesterday, indeed of all the past years.

And so we are responsible for sin—yet in the grip of sin— all our lives long. Many Biblical scholars believe that St. Paul, in his famous cry of anguish about the other law in his members, was reflecting his experience *after* his conversion. In other words, he is not saying that he was once in this

situation but now as a Christian he is not. If anything, as a
Christian the tension is greater because the Christian learns
how high God's law is, how searching His judgments. It is
as a Christian that one really knows to what an extent he has
"not done those things which he ought to have done," and
"done those things which he ought not to have done." So St.
Paul's concluding question is not "Who did deliver me?" but
"Who *will* deliver me from the body of this death?" or to
translate the Greek more pointedly, "Who will keep on
delivering me?"

Then no matter how marked or how undramatic one's conversion, or first awareness of God's forgiving power, this is
only the beginning of a relationship in which again and
again we see ourselves as in the wrong, again and again
acknowledge the fact, over and over know the relief of God's
taking our sins away. Over and over again we see ourselves
as unacceptable and then know God's free acceptance—and
thus re-accept ourselves.

The confidence that we are in this continuing relationship
—sin or no—is one of the greatest comforts of the Christian
life. Those who live simply on an ethical plane are often
driven into sin by the despair born of wrong already done,
just as the errant husband who cannot face the judgment em-
bodied in his virtuous wife, returns again to other arms which
welcome. This is because sin is separation and in our despair
at being cut off from the right sources of meaning we cling to
the little meanings. And, too, our resentment of that from
which we are separated makes us rebellious and moves us to
obstinate persistence in evil. So St. Paul knew and could say,
"I had not known sin, but by the law" (Rom. 7:7) and com-
plained, "Sin taking occasion by the commandment, wrought
in me all manner of concupiscence" (Rom. 7:8). Now this *is*
in the past tense. No one who has ever really experienced the
acceptance which comes when God "has broken every barrier down" and removed the separation sin brings, will choose

more sin as his comfort in a state of separation. The continuing basis of relationship is what gave Luther the temerity to say what has been so often misunderstood: *Pecca fortiter,* Sin bravely—to which he adds: "but believe more bravely still."

But these very words may evoke from a sensitive reader an objection that probably has been taking shape all along: "That's the trouble with this whole business. If a man knows he can accept himself on such easy terms, he will go on doing wrong." Yes, in all probability he will go on doing wrong. But so will the man who stands "on his merits." The question is: is it more or less likely that a man will reform when he lives by the grace of forgiveness? Of course, for the question to make sense we must stick to the same man. John Jones, who asks no gift of acceptance from God, may be a more ethical person than George Smith, who is forgiven daily; but the real question is, would Jones be an even more ethical person—or less so—if he let God be the source of his self-acceptance? and, would Smith be a more decent fellow—or an even less decent one—if he did not count on God?

The answer to this question will serve as a review of some matters already discussed and at the same time introduce two important points not yet considered.

All men sin, and if a man is simply going to try to live by the rules he will have to rationalize his faults or else suffer a sense of guilt. If he does the first, he will harm his inner life, thus increasing its propensity for evil power over the whole man, and he eliminates the tension so fruitful for improvement. On the other hand, if he does not rationalize and if he retains his self-criticism, he loses self-acceptance, is consciously unhappy, is without that confidence in oneself which makes for goodness and effective action, and he may be led into one of a dozen "opiates" to ease his suffering.

Now, what if the same man should be living in the pattern of daily judgment and forgiveness? He will still fall short of God's whole law—maybe rather conspicuously, but there are at least six wholesome factors at work: First, he *knows* he falls short. Second, he no longer needs to rationalize: he is freed from the tedious and nerve-racking chore of making up reasons and defenses for every shortcoming. In turn, this means, third, that he will more naturally and spontaneously admit his fault to others (instead of the usually unsuccessful cover-up.) Fourth, he will have the peace and effectiveness of accepting himself. Fifth, he has a clearer conception of what lines his reform should take. And sixth, he has a well-spring of action to this end. This last calls for special attention, because it, more than anything else, accounts for the fact that the man who really has his status by grace and not by works can do better works.

We do good things from a variety of motives. Suppose I am seen opening my wallet and giving a five-dollar bill to a needy person leaving my office. As to motivation (conscious or unconscious), this can mean a number of things: (1) that I wished my associates to note my generosity; (2) that I decided this would be a quicker way to deal with the man than to go into his problem more deeply and work out permanent solutions for his needy condition; (3) that I hoped he would do me a favor, such as speaking well of my deed; (4) that it made me feel good to do a creditable good work; (5) that it would help make up for the fact that I had slighted someone yesterday; or (6) that I was grateful for the many blessings that had come to me in times of need. A superficial reaction to this kind of analysis might be: "What does all this introspection matter, if the man gets the five dollars?" But the ethical concern of Christianity is twofold: first, that we have good deeds; second, that we have good people—and the second is the more important in the long run. In the illustration, I am a better man if operating under the last two of the possible motivations than if actuated by any of the first four. But there's also a vast difference in the moral quality between the fifth and sixth motivations. To do something to try to put myself in the right is quite a different thing from doing something because I am grateful that I, too, have received unearned favors.

The distinction is even sharper when it bears on our relationship to God. To do good in order to try to earn favor or status with God (even assuming that one can do this—and we have seen above that one can't) is prudential rather than ethical, and while the action may involve present sacrifice, it is really done in terms of a selfishness that "takes the long view." But to do God's will because of gratitude to Him for His constant forgiveness, to seek to be more acceptable to Him in gratitude for the fact that He accepts us, to seek to *be* that which He has *taken us for,* namely, righteous—this is a motivation for goodness which has no "angle," with man or with God, and is a mirror of the pure love of God for us.

This motivation is also of a higher quality because it saves us from both pride and false humility. Obviously pride is a sin and humility is a virtue. Yet pride is a sin which cannot be abolished directly and humility is a virtue which cannot be achieved directly: the attainment of humility as a virtue automatically defeats itself, because then we have something to be proud of. This attitude toward humility can be illustrated by the story of the Carthusian who was explaining to a stranger the ethos of his little-known Order. "As for learning, we're not to be compared with the Jesuits," he said. "When it comes to good works, we don't match the Franciscans. As to preaching, we're not in a class with the Dominicans. But," he concluded, "when it comes to humility, we're tops."

Now, pride as to one's natural gifts or achievements may be offensive, but not nearly so offensive as pride as to one's goodness or religiousness, that is, as to one's status with God. The remedy both for false humility and for pride is much the same. In the case of the appraisal of our natural gifts and our accomplishments, the answer is not to deny that we have gifts or that we have accomplished anything. If such denials are insincerely made, then they are hypocritical; if they are sincerely made, then they are misleading, both to ourselves and to others whom our gifts might profit. The answer is to recognize throughout the *sources* of our gifts and of all those factors which have played their part in our accomplishments. Here we can readily enough see how much we owe to parents and teachers and to many factors not of our own making, and back of it all, to God, "from whom cometh every good and perfect gift."

The same is true of the appraisal of our spiritual state. If we are living the Christian life, there is no use in denying our status as accepted of God, but it is important to remember the source of that status. It is ours, not through our own merits but through God's free gift.

Thus we see that the real opposite of pride is gratitude, not humility. Humility is the fruit of gratitude, and humility so resulting cannot possibly give ground for new pride, on the one hand; nor will it, on the other, interfere with the quite proper joy as to our status with God as Christians, and our quite appropriate witness to the same in personal terms.

The reason why the members of the more conventional denominations have generally hesitated to witness to the fact that they are Christians or the fact that they have been converted is not only a matter of "good taste" and reticence to press one's religious position upon others: it is also due to a false assumption that to claim to be a Christian or to be converted means to claim that one lives up to the high ethical code of Jesus' teaching. Naturally, anyone should be reticent about claiming to be a Christian upon these terms. But if we recognize that the Christian is not the good man but the man who knows he is not good and knows that the basis of his self-acceptance is the fact that God freely accepts him though unacceptable, then there is certainly no pride in witnessing to the fact that one is a Christian. If he understands the Christian doctrine of salvation, what he is witnessing to is that he is a sinner and that God is good.

We can see, then, that a deed done from the motivation of gratitude to God is religiously and ethically superior to the identical deed done from any other motive. But we can go further than this and say that even in terms of getting good deeds done, gratitude is, by and large, the most effective motivation. Were Christian ethics essentially the keeping of a defined code, then the motive of earning God's favor might work about as well as gratitude. However, what the Christian law for life calls for is, as we have seen, an imaginative ethic which goes way beyond fixed rules of behavior, to include spontaneous response in love to *ad hoc* needs as they present themselves. What is needed for this kind of performance is a motivation that is "on tap" and under high pressure; otherwise, the opportunity for service will pass us by and the spirit in which the personal encounter is met will often fail in love. The needs of men will often not tarry (for example, speaking the right word just when another person needs it) while we check a code of ethics in our mind and calculate what our duty is. A good thing done for another which carries with it the feeling that we are doing it to do a good thing, or "in order to" reform the other, or to receive a response of gratitude back, betrays by its very timbre the calculatedness in motivation. Goodness to the other because of the other's need of our goodness brings a convincing freshness with it, and, in fact, is much more likely to produce the right response in the other because there is no "in order to" wrapped up in the package. Now it happens that this very kind of ethical action is the reflection of the way God is to us; hence it "comes natural" to those who know themselves so treated by God.

Our openness as a conduit for this love of God (by which we are accepted, and in grateful response to which we accept others) will be impeded, in the life of the Christian, by the plain fact that the good often does not seem as attractive to us as the evil. "Ideals" can sometimes be very cold company. It is often only through a very vivid sense of serving a Person, rather than serving an ideal, that we can be brought to make the right choices as increasingly this devotion to a Person leads us to *want* to do the right. This will reduce much of our inner tension as more and more our whole will is in the same direction.

This end in human personality is what St. Augustine was summing up in his dictum, "Love God and do what you please." If we really love God, with our whole minds, our whole hearts, our whole souls, our whole strength, then above all else we will want to do that which pleases God. That the grace of God, following on the judgment of God, can effect in us a gratitude which moves us to want to do what God wants, is something to which almost any Christian can testify; that his whole life and personality is so transformed, few would dare to think. But the degree to which that is so is the degree to which we have entered our heritage as "sons of God and fellow-heirs of Christ" and this is the degree to which we are living in the Spirit. This is the clue to the psychology of St. Paul's affirmation, ". . . it is no longer I who live, but Christ who lives in me; and the life I now live in the flesh I live by faith in the Son of God, who loved me and gave himself for me" (Gal. 2:20).

# Chapter V

## *INHIBITION*

WHAT WE HAVE been talking about in the last chapter is how to handle real guilt. In this connection we have seen that one of the ways these days that men rationalize their guilt is to label it a "guilt-complex" or "guilt consciousness." But such words do stand for something real. There can be a devastating sense of guilt when, in fact, there is no guilt. This can take many erratic forms which are pathological. No attempt will be made to treat these here. But there is one type of guilt-complex which is so widespread and so typical in American life that it forms a significant part of our anxiety and it is one for the healing of which there clearly are resources in the Christian Faith. I refer to the widespread feeling that the joys of the flesh are sinful, or less worthy than more "spiritual" activity.

The reader may immediately assume that this chapter is meant for members of those Churches who center their conception of sin around strictures against sex, drinking, dancing, smoking, and cards. Would that this problem were only theirs! Unfortunately the notions which have brought forth such explicit strictures are more widespread. Actually the devaluation of the flesh has found its way into the unconscious of most Americans to such an extent that even people who are very "emancipated" are burdened internally by a peculiar sense of uneasiness about all such matters. It has formed a part of the "racial unconscious." In our culture it has had such disparate results as grave difficulty in sexual

44

adjustment in marriage and a heightened sense of excitement about, and an undue focus upon, sensual enjoyment.

The psychology of the matter can be better understood if we consider briefly the sources of the attitude and then survey some of its characteristic expressions. Here we get a clear example of the fact that bad theology makes for bad life. The trouble lies in the view taken toward the distinction between soul and body. If man is both spiritual and material in his total make-up—and that he is, is obvious—then it is difficult not to use such words as "soul" and "body." But when men have used them they have tended to identify the soul with *good* and the body with *evil*. Now there is evil in the world and evil in human life and men have quite properly wished to eradicate it, both in general and in themselves. And they have often assumed that if they were more soul and less body or if spiritual joys could replace bodily joys, then evil would be constrained.

This assumption figured large in the theology of our Puritan forefathers. They were not entirely consistent in it: rum and "bundling" were characteristic parts of early life in New England. It awaited a later generation to substitute grape juice in the Lord's Supper, with an abstemiousness which did not mark the Founder of the Supper. But soon another movement which church historians call "pietism" swept the country—among those of Anglo-Saxon roots in the expression of Wesleyan "perfectionism," and among the immigrants of German origin in terms of the pietistic revival which had already made its mark in recent decades in the homeland. Later, from quite a different source, those holding the views of unreformed medieval Catholicism contributed their own share of the under-rating of the flesh, with a conviction that chastity is "a higher life" than marriage and that "self-denial" of fleshly joys is as such pleasing to God. Neither social historian nor theologian could parcel out the responsibility for an attitude that has formed a part of our inheritance, which can be summed up as *the more soul and the less body, the better*. Composite as the sources are and divergent as are the particular applications made by various groups today, nevertheless there has spread to all of us a malignant psychical deformation which results in anxiety and unwholesomeness.

The results are different in the case of those who feel a moral imperative and strive to do right according to their religious convictions, and in the case of those who feel "emancipated" from such claims. But in either case the results are unfortunate.

As to the latter, the actual indulging of the flesh creates conflict patterns which interfere with the joy which they so eagerly seek; at the same time a sense of guilt adds a certain "spice" to sensual enjoyment which often makes its pursuit inordinate and out of all proportion to life as a whole. These folks have been thoroughly taught in our American culture that spirit and flesh are separate and, forced to a choice, they have chosen the flesh. Lost then is the spiritual meaning of fleshly expression, and with it the restraints and integration which the spirit could bring.

As for those who are dedicated to spirit the results are also unfortunate. Restraining themselves they avoid the enjoyment of the flesh, and three interesting results follow: a narrowing of the scope of life (a sort of "drying up"), a thoroughgoing resentment that they are so denied, and a compensating pride in their righteous condition. This is perhaps the principal reason why in many communities the "religious" people seem to be the most boring and unpleasant in the community. Thus both those who choose flesh and those who choose spirit lose out and fall short of receiving the promise of Him Who said, "I am come that they might have life, and that they might have it more abundantly."

The healing of both classes of people is somewhat hampered by the presence of the other group in the community.

The "spiritual" people hesitate to relax the prohibitions because all too evident all around them is the disorder in the lives of those who have. On the other hand, the other group hesitate to introduce a spiritual dimension which could bring order into their lives because all too evident around them is the joylessness and dullness of so many of those who do take religion seriously. Both groups thus agree on one point: that being religious means less joy in life. So one group foregoes the joy, the other foregoes religion.

Both are wrong. The only remedy for either outlook is a thoroughgoing re-thinking of the relation of spirit and flesh, of soul and body. Since most people who devaluate the flesh think that they ground their views on the Bible, especially on St. Paul, perhaps it would be best to start there.

There are two Greek words which correspond to our English word "flesh." They are *soma* and *sarx*. In the King James Version the first is usually translated "body" and the second "flesh." *Soma* is a neutral word and there is no passage in which it is found in a condemnatory sense or is set in opposition to spirit. It is the word *sarx* that is found in such passages as "I keep under my body, and bring it into subjection . . ." (I Cor. 9:27). Now what does *sarx* mean precisely? The best clue we can gain from the passage in which St. Paul lists "the works of the flesh":

> . . . the works of the flesh are plain: immorality, impurity, licentiousness, idolatry, sorcery, enmity, strife, jealousy, anger, selfishness, dissension, party spirit, envy, drunkenness, carousing, and the like (Gal. 5:19-21).

Now what is common to these sins? The use of the body? No, because idolatry, sorcery, enmity, strife, jealousy, anger, selfishness, dissension, party spirit, and envy are obviously states of mind, sins of the spirit. What is common to all of them, including the more "fleshly" sounding sins (such as licentiousness and drunkenness) is wrong intention in the spirit, a wrong spiritual direction, the downward destructive tendencies in man. For the implementation of these tendencies the body, of course, can be used (for example, even in as spiritual a sin as "envy" the body can be used to make the malice felt). From this we can see that what is essentially wrong with lust is not that the body is used carnally but that the situation is such, the human relations are such, that this particular use of the body is the implementation of a wrong spirit.

Therefore it is not right to assume that the body is bad and that the spirit is good and that the less of body in life and the more of spirit the better a man will be. The body is never bad, the spirit often is. All sin is spirit gone wrong. Indeed the sins which Jesus regarded as the worst are the ones most obviously connected with spirit: pride, contempt of one's fellow man, calculatedness, etc.

But to affirm that the body is not bad, nor the source of sin, is not to state the full Christian understanding of the matter. There is a more positive foundation for a joyful relationship to the world. Early in Christian history the Church was faced with the contentions of those who would identify evil with the material order. So that they could save God from having created the material order, which was assumed to be evil, the Gnostics assigned the task of creation to the outermost of the various emanations of God. Manicheanism (of which St. Augustine was a devotee before his conversion to Christianity) went still further: the creation of the world was assigned to a God of evil, the creation of spirit to a God of good. In rejecting all such positions, Christianity affirmed the Biblical faith that God created the world and *all that therein is*. Since God cannot create evil, that means that the material order is good. So we read in Genesis: "And God saw everything that he had made, and, behold, it was very good." Evil in the world there is, sin in the world there is; but these are not because of the material order. All sin partakes of the character of the first sin, as seen in the Edenic myth: "And the serpent said to Eve, 'Ye shall be as gods.'" Sin arises when spirit gets things in the wrong proportion, affirms the wrong loyalties, distorts man's purposes. If we take seriously the Biblical doctrine of creation, we will not only not say that the flesh is evil; we will also not say the flesh is neutral. We must affirm that *the flesh is good*. And what was good enough for God to create is good enough for us to enjoy.

Not only this; the creative order is continually related to God as a sign of His presence, as the means through which His ends are effectuated through the free co-operation of men. This is a sacramental universe. The evolved things are the outward and visible signs of the inward and spiritual Grace which evolved them. Thus in receiving the world gratefully we receive Him Who made it and makes it. Rejoicing in the flesh, we yield praise to Him Whose joy it is to further our joy. When we think of the relationship of God to His own world we gain a clue to the real norm of goodness. Genuine fulfillment under God is the proper sacramental relationship of spirit to flesh, the use of flesh in such a way as properly to express spirit and be a means thereto.

Contrary to the religious notions of so many people whose Christianity has included a heresy on the doctrine of creation, we can affirm that *spirit is not better than flesh; the true good is spirit and flesh properly integrated, sacramentally united*. The true end of man is not spiritual, it is *psychosomatic*, i.e., soul-body. This is why the doctrine that the Church proclaims about the ultimate meaning of life is not the immortality of the soul but the resurrection of the body, that is, the continuity of the total personality, with appropriate means of expression, communication and inter-relatedness. We shall consider this more fully in Chapter IX, but meanwhile it is enough to say that even in the life to come we do not anticipate disembodied spirituality nor should we value such now.

Let us apply these principles to the matter of sex. When young people are raised with the notion that sex is bad, nasty and "unclean," whatever this may accomplish in terms of chastity in their youth, they are often crippled for proper sexual adjustment in marriage. When they are married it is now as though they had a special dispensation to do what is essentially a bad thing. Their conscious minds may tell them better; but in marriage the physical experience is obviously much the same as that which heretofore had been conceived of as bad, and the fact of a marriage ceremony cannot be relied upon to eradicate from the unconscious mind a long-established sense of guilt about the whole thing. The results are more devastating in the case of women than in the case of men due to the traditional weight that the racial unconscious has put upon women to maintain purity. And hence to this factor we can trace a good deal of the difficulty of mutuality of fulfillment in sexual intercourse.

On the other hand, if we view the sexual relationship as a beautiful and good thing which God has rejoiced to provide for our joy, then we will not tell young people not to engage in it because it is sensual, fleshly and unclean, but rather we will tell them that they should not do it because it is so good a thing that they should not use it except when it can be used sacramentally, that is, as the outward and visible sign of an inward and spiritual grace. Since that which it is the sign of is the yielding of one to the other in totality of spirit and meaning, the pooling of hopes and fears, of strength and weakness, on the basis of abiding trust and commitment to each other, these right conditions can only exist in the case of marriage. Hence its use apart from marriage is not the doing of a bad thing, but the using of a good

thing *sacrilegiously*. The service of Holy Communion provides an analogy. If someone went up to the rail at Com-
munion-time simply to find out whether port or sherry was
being used, we would not conclude that the sacrament was
a bad thing, but that he had used the sacrament sacrilegiously.

This approach gives a positive reason for chastity at the
proper time of one's life and at the same time unbinds the
strictures which restrain the full joy in marriage in a relationship in which there are no nice things and not-nice
things, nothing clean or unclean, no limits to the possibilities
of an ecstasy which is both spiritual and physical, which is
psychosomatic, which is sacramental.

This approach also gives a clue to the proper place of
sexual intercourse within marriage—a problem often over-
looked in the concentration of interest in the propriety of
extra-marital relationships. Just as the marriage license does
not make what was up to then bad suddenly good, but rather
provides an opportunity for a good thing to be used in a good
way, so too the marriage license does not make every use of
this good thing a good use. Within a marriage it is possible
for the partners to "use" each other as a physical conven-
ience in which spiritual expression is not lined up with the
physical activity. It is in these terms that we must answer
the question often asked—one which can be answered to no
satisfaction legalistically or even medically, namely, what is
the proper frequency of intercourse within a marriage? The
failure to have spiritual commitment express itself adequately in physical terms is inhibition; physical expression
not related to a total soul-body meaning is *inordinateness*,
which means literally "not in order," that is, "out of order."
There is no pat answer to the question. The problem being
a sacramental one, we must take into account the fact that
a sacrament is both the expression of a spiritual reality and
the means thereto; thus it is important that neither spirit nor

flesh should get too far out ahead of the other. Inhibition and inordinateness are at root the same thing: the discorrelation of spirit and flesh.

This discorrelation is especially seen in the ways two classes of people handle the matter of alcohol. Now it is true that in the case of alcoholic beverages we are dealing with something which is not "natural" in the sense that the sexual relationship is, but rather with something that represents the work of man's ingenuity upon the natural. But those who would press this distinction in order to rule out the use of alcohol prove entirely too much. Ruled out also would be soap, contraception, medicine, machinery. The Biblical doctrine of creation must be interpreted in the light of the Biblical doctrine of man as the image of God and as sharing in God's creation, even to the extent of bringing to greater perfection natural possibilities. Fermentation and distillation are among the more interesting of these possibilities. The resulting alcoholic beverages are not evil in themselves any more than nuclear fission is evil in itself.

The evaluation has to be made in larger terms. St. Paul hardly recognized the optimum possibilities of the matter in his word, "a little wine is good for the stomach." The kind of hypocrisy such an approach can engender is symbolized by the place of Lydia Pinkham's remedies in the history of American culture. Somewhat more imaginative is the Psalmist, when he says, "He causeth the grass to grow for the cattle, and herb for the service of man . . . and wine that maketh glad the heart of man . . ." (Ps. 104:14-15). The cocktail hour can be a time of real renewal: we can be lifted out of the ruts into which the day has taken us, our imaginations can be inspired, our vision cleared. This gift can help break down the barriers between people, can make introverts more extrovert. A martini before dinner can put a new face on things, enabling those who have evening tasks to approach them with more freshness. Steins of beer can enhance the late evening college "bull-session." Just the right wine can dignify a course at dinner and play its part in the glory of an evening.

Yet this same thing is the instrument of the devil. No one of us has to look very far, perhaps not even beyond the members of our families, to see drink as the means of the destruction of personality, the deflection of fine intentions, the ravager of home life. It is quite understandable that many people have decided that liquor is bad, or that it is more bad than good; and it is equally easy to understand why those whose drinking schedule is limited, do it on a basis that a little bit of something bad won't hurt them too much. It is easy to understand why some Churches have erected the evil of drink into a dogma as significant to them as the Incarnation or the Atonement, and why some Christians would sooner have their minister deny the divinity of Christ than to be seen with a glass of beer.

Those who conceive of liquor itself as bad, tend to conceive of the problem of alcoholism in a quite simple way. One drink is bad, two drinks are worse; one drink is a sin, two drinks are two sins; and people who sin impressively in this regard pay for it: truly the wages of sin is death. Here modern psychology and that great enterprise known as Alcoholics Anonymous help us to see the problem on a somewhat more profound level, by asking not *how much* or even *whether*, but *why*. Why does the alcoholic drink? Once we ask the right question, the answer becomes fairly obvious— and we can test it in terms of nearly any alcoholic we know well. Almost invariably an alcoholic drinks because of some deeper problem, some problem of the spirit. Again we see the source of fleshly inordinateness in the spirit, not in the flesh. It is *sarx*, namely, the disorientation of the spirit, of the inner life, that is the trouble. Alcohol is merely the escape mechanism by which a person temporarily rises above

—or numbs himself to—a painful tension, an unresolved conflict, a major inadequacy or vacuum in the spiritual life.

The problems for which alcohol could be used as an escape are as varied as the individuals who have them. They can be any of the types of problems which form the chapter headings of this book. Even if we can find some way to stop a man from drinking we do not thereby heal the man. This does not mean that we should not seek to stop his drinking. A drunken driver is dangerous regardless of the state of his complexes. Further, we will never get at his complexes as long as he continues in a state of escape; and physical well-being, which can be in part restored when the bottle is taken away, is a great factor in the restoration of mental well-being. But that the removal of a particular escape device does not solve the problem from which a man is escaping is evident if we remember that other things than alcohol can serve a similar function. Some people hide from their problems by hyper-activity. "Never a dull moment" as the motif of a person's life is almost a sure sign that a person is keeping his conscious mind filled so that he will not observe the chasm beneath. As we have seen in the analysis of the way we handle our guilt, we *must* feel right about ourselves; and distraction, though less socially dangerous than excessive drinking, can be as much a sign of an unhealthy personality. Some women when unhappy go out and buy a new hat. Though more expensive in one way, and less in another, than five old-fashioneds, the psychology is much the same. These days the couch is part of the liturgical apparatus of the priesthood of psychoanalysis, and it is sound liturgics: before inner problems can be dealt with the patient must relax the pressures which keep the true self from being evident. The doctor must remove the bandage before he can treat the wound.

This brief digression into the matter of escape-mechanisms generally is intended to focus our attention on the *why* in connection with drinking, before the questions *whether* or *how much* are asked. It shows that we are not here dealing with a wrong thing, but with a matter of the spirit—which could be wrong or right. If the general orientation of the spirit is right, then we can turn our attention to the next two questions and view them in much the same way as we have looked at the matter of sex. The question is one of the total well-being of a psychosomatic relationship. Some persons who have straightened out their spiritual problems may still refrain from alcohol because they know from experience that a chain reaction is set up in them by even a single drink, which starts the vicious circle toward the disruption of spiritual soundness no less than of bodily well-being. These are "alcoholics" in the sense in which the word is used of the members of a group like Alcoholics Anonymous. (Their sound understanding of the matter is indicated by the fact that there is no alliance between A.A. and W.C.T.U. Those who argue that people of sobriety should abstain because some people get drunk do not deny themselves automobiles because of the deaths and injuries caused by bad drivers.) On the other hand, a person well-directed in spirit may begin the evening to be spent with his family and friends with refreshment which may well, in limited sense, be viewed as an "escape," that is, a way of helping to turn his mind away from various pressing problems of the day so that he may enter more fully into the life that is around him, and thus come back to his problems with a renewed perspective. In other words, even escape can have its place in a well-ordered life.

In these terms, the question of *how much* is no different than the question of how much food one should eat: it is not a question of the less sin the better—a view we would never take toward food—but rather a question of proportion in terms of one's total responsibilities. The grounding of this attitude will be discussed more fully in the next chapter, where we will see the implications of the Christian doctrine of vocation, which provides the basis for the imposition of proper limits, or the acceptance of limits which we cannot help, upon our use of those things which are attractive to us.

Now, of course, taste as well as responsibility enters in. Some people just don't happen to like alcoholic beverages. Sometimes the dislike is the conscious expression of what in the unconscious is really inhibition; sometimes it is not. If not, there is nothing unhealthy about abstinence. One is reminded of the answer the Episcopal priest gave a Baptist lady who asked if the Episcopal Church believed in smoking. "Yes," he said, "but not as generally necessary to salvation" (echoing the catechism distinction between the greater and lesser sacraments). Just as in the case of the alcoholic the question is *why,* not *whether,* so in the case of the non-drinker, the important question is *why not,* not *whether.*

There are a number of *good* reasons not to. An alcoholic knows from experience that one drink is likely to "set him off." So he doesn't drink at all. Or a man's financial situation may be such that a glass of ale for him may mean no glass of milk for his child (but note: the same will be true of sirloin steak—recognized by most "drys" as a good thing). Or a man may decide that he should give up cocktails and give the money for some worth-while cause (but note: he could with equal reasonableness decide not to ride Pullman any more or buy a cheaper car next time; it's a matter of priority of claims, not of "good" or "bad"). Finally, a man may have adopted a habit of life, an integrated pattern of duties and pleasures, of times and places, in which drinking has no place. As long as he doesn't look down upon those whose round of life is different (in the spirit of the Pharisee's "Thank God I am not as other men"), then there is no reason why he should reopen the question with himself every time he is offered a drink.

If the place of drinking in our everyday lives, if it is to have a place, is settled along these lines, we will be saved from both inhibition and inordinateness. If a person does not drink, it is important that he not drink for the right reasons. It is important for the total meaning of his personality that it be on the positive grounds of vocation or taste rather than the negative ground of inhibition. On the other hand, if one does drink (assuming now a proper proportion of things) it is important that it be on the right grounds also; it is not healthy for him to view it as "a concession to the flesh," and it is too minimal for him to view it merely as a means (neutral in itself) to certain spiritual ends; he should be able to rejoice in the goodness of this fruit of God's and man's joint creativity. We praise God for the wheat, and at the same time are grateful for the miller and the baker. We should praise God for the grape and at the same time honor the vintner.

To recapitulate: The things of the flesh are not only not bad, they are not even simply neutral. They are good— though in our use of them our spirits are by no means always good. If a man attempts to justify the time he spends in playing golf on the ground that he does it for the exercise or for making business contacts, you might think him hypocritical; but if we thought he really meant it, we would worry about him more: it is good to do things simply because they are fun as well as because they contribute to some other specific need of the personal or social situation. Having fun is itself a need of the human personality.

The validation of earthly joys and the grateful acceptance of them is grounded in the Biblical doctrine we affirm in the Creed when we call God "maker of Heaven *and earth*." This is the Christian answer to the problem of inhibition.

# Chapter VI

## *FRUSTRATION*

But what if things are such that you can't enjoy certain aspects of life? Suppose a fine young lady with all the natural impulses toward marriage and a family doesn't seem to meet "the right person" . . . and years go by. A husband would like to provide a better home and more of "the good things of life" for himself and his family but can't seem to get ahead in spite of his most assiduous efforts. To these examples we can add even more obvious ones of illness, physical disability and tragic misfortune which hem in life and narrow its possibilities.

People differ widely in their reaction to the same types of limitation. It is wrong to assume, as we sometimes do, sympathetically, that cripples are persons of inspiring character. Some are and some aren't; some are serene and towers of strength to others; some are crotchety, and a spiritual, no less than a material, burden on others. Thus we cannot make a direct correlation between limitation and frustration. *Frustration does not come from having limitations; it comes from a wrong spiritual orientation to one's limitations.* What is the factor that makes the difference between the occupant of a wheel chair who radiates a depth of joy and warmth toward others and one who displays bitterness and despair? What is the factor which makes the difference between a single woman in her thirties who is obviously confident and happy and one who is obsessed with her lonely state?

It is important to discard a wrong answer first. Simple an-

swers are not always the best. Some people faced with tragedy piously say, "Well, it's the will of God, and I must bear
it." As we shall see, there is a stage in the matter when
something like this can be said. But to start there is wrong
both psychologically and religiously. It is psychologically
wrong because it cuts the nerve of thoughtful and strenuous
action to change the situation insofar as is humanly possible, and because it is either the expression of, or the foundation for, a "martyr-complex." It is religiously bad, being both
presumptuous and blasphemous. It is presumptuous because
no one can speak with such certainty about what the will of
God is in a given situation. It is blasphemous because it at-
tributes to God purposes which we would not respect even
in an earthly parent. In fact the comparison is supposed to
be in reverse: Jesus said, "If ye then, being evil, know how
to give good gifts unto your children; how much more shall
your heavenly Father . . ." (Luke 11:13). God does not
willingly hurt the sons of men. To the statement, "It must
have been the will of God that my boy be killed in the war,"
the only answer fair to God and realistic to the facts is, "As
a matter of circumstances, it was the will of the enemy
machine-gunner and back of him the will of wicked men"
(a category not necessarily limited to the enemy government, but including all men who had a part in the causes
of the war). We can't saddle God with that one nor can we
blame on God (whether piously or resentfully) the heart
attack of a man who was working too hard and who was
forty pounds overweight. As we learn more about the psychosomatic causes of diseases which we once thought were
purely fortuitous physical derangements, we should sufficiently respect the mystery of those factors in life we do not
fully understand, to hesitate to make a simple attribution to
God of what well may have resulted from human will—directly or indirectly.

But what we do *within* the given limitations—brought

about by our own fault, the fault of others, or otherwise—does have to do very definitely with the will of God. And the reason we have gotten the impression that God wills the evil is that the saints have generally made such a good show of turning sows' ears into silk purses, have produced such amazing goodness out of evil situations, that we have turned around and credited God with the evil that made possible so much good. But this is to bring God in at the wrong point. He is to be credited with the grace and power which redeemed the evil, and produced the greater good in the lives of His saints, but this is in terms of what they did *within* the limitations, following His leading.

This is nowhere better illustrated than in the life of Samuel Schereschewsky. A rabbinical student in Russian Lithuania, Schereschewsky came across a Hebrew translation of the New Testament and was set to thinking about the possibility that Jesus really was the Messiah of his people. His spiritual quest led him to Germany for study and subsequently to New York City, where he eventually prepared for the priesthood of the Episcopal Church at the General Theological Seminary. His brilliance was such that there it was intimated to him that he might look forward to joining the faculty; but at this time he was very much influenced by one of the first missionaries to China, Bishop Boone, and he decided to join him and use his linguistic abilities to translate the Scriptures into Chinese. He set sail, learning the Chinese language during the voyage (which, of course, took longer in those days).

Early in his career we can see something of Schereschewsky's constructive way of dealing with limitations. Word reached him that a fine young lady from Brooklyn, who had been described in glowing terms, was going to join the Mission. She was staying in Shanghai; he was in Pekin, nine hundred miles away. The winter weather made travel by boat impossible except for the last two hundred miles; so he walked the first seven hundred. Upon departing he told his companion he was going to Shanghai to get married. His engagement was announced two weeks after his arrival. (We see here no "It's the will of God that I be alone out here"!)

Schereschewsky felt strongly that the most important thing to be done in the missionary enterprise was the translation of the Scriptures into the native tongue. So when he was elected Bishop of the missionary area by the American House of Bishops, he declined. However, when he was elected again he reluctantly accepted—though he afterwards sought to withdraw his acceptance and five years later expressed the hope that the Church would permit him to resign and resume his work of translation. Then one day he suffered a sunstroke and became almost totally paralyzed—save for the middle finger on the right hand. Forced to return to America, he immediately set to work to complete his work of translation. Since no Chinese scholar was available to serve as scribe and he was unable to write himself, Schereschewsky poked out on a typewriter with his one finger the English equivalents of the Chinese characters; and so eager was he to push on with the work that when his one active finger would grow tired he would stamp out the letters with a small stick clutched in his fist. He produced two translations, one in Mandarin for the common man, one in Easy Wenli for the educated. He set sail with his manuscript to China, where, with the aid of Chinese assistants, he published the manuscript and then proceeded to prepare reference Bibles in each of the dialects. One week after he brought this work to a close, he died—a fulfillment of his prayer: "I am never without pain . . . when I have done this book I pray the dear Lord to take me to Himself." Schereschewsky thus provided tools which set forward the whole missionary effort —of course, quite beyond the limits of his own Church—

much more than his own individual leadership in the mission field could have done. And he was grateful that he had been enabled, because of his paralysis, to complete the really important thing. He was able to say: "I have sat in this chair for over twenty years. It seemed very hard at first. But God knew best. He kept me for the work for which I am best fitted." It is in this way that one can properly talk about the will of God in connection with confining circumstances.

It is not the broad river that turns the turbine; it is the water rushing through the narrowed gorge. The latter does not create the power, either; there must be a turbine there. In personal life, what is this turbine? The clearest image of what it is is Jesus Christ on the Cross of Calvary. Life was certainly hemmed in for Him. Because God leaves men free they are enabled even to close the Lord of the Universe out of His world. In the words of Cecil Alexander,

> 'His are the thousand sparkling rills
> That from a thousand fountains burst,
> And fill with music all the hills;
> And yet he saith, I thirst.

The hands which were active in the healing of men were now nailed down to the wood of the Cross; feet which were accustomed to visit haunts of need were now securely held. He was not only hemmed in physically; He was closed in upon spiritually. Unresponsiveness was at its maximum all around: Pharisees and Sadducees who heretofore had been divided by their quarrels were united in their hate of Him: Roman and Jew, generally at swords' points, gladly collaborated for this deed. An atmosphere of hate and malice and cynicism almost engulfed Him. Well-furnished with enemies, He was bereft of His friends, even His closest ones. Closed out also, it would seem, was any chance for the fulfillment of the great hopes with which He had inspired men's hearts. So great seemed His defeat that a few days later, on the road to Emmaus, two of His disciples could say sadly, "We had thought that it was He who would save Israel." What a setting for frustration! Yet, from that Cross have streamed power and healing, light and salvation unto the ends of the earth. More has been accomplished for the good of man by His work in those closing hours than by the most free and active endeavor of anyone at any time in his life in all history. And His spiritual activity during those hours included also the immediate: He prayed for His persecutors ("Father, forgive them; for they know not what they do."); He redeemed a dying thief for eternal life ("Today shalt thou be with me in paradise."); He made arrangements with John for His mother's care ("Woman, behold thy son! Behold thy mother!"). But supremely He reveals to us what it is that marks the difference, in the same circumstances of life, between frustration and spiritual power and confidence: "Father, into Thy hands I commend my spirit."

This is the answer. If we think we live for ourselves and that we are the ultimate end of our existence, then confinement necessarily means frustration. If we see ourselves as servants of God, meant to be used by Him, through our free co-operation, for His work in the world, then any set of circumstances can provide a matrix for meaningful action and a sense of significance in our daily moments. This is Christ's message from the Cross; this by reflection is the clue to the life of Bishop Schereschewsky, His servant. This is the key to the same problem today.

How important a key it is! For if confinement and limitation in a life is to mean frustration, then, indeed, we all must be frustrated. There are some things that I can do well; there are others that I can do, but not well; and there are many things that I cannot do at all. And this is true of every reader. We are finite; more than that, the actions of others (sometimes right, sometimes wrong) hem us in; and our own past actions (right ones as well as sinful ones) hem us in. There is no one who would not be frustrated if limitation and frustration were co-terminous. Hence, the importance of the *Christian doctrine of vocation.* This principle is that the meaning of our existence is no less than the fulfillment of the task of being co-sharers in God's triune work in the world, His *creative, redemptive,* and *community-making* activity. In other words, the nature of God Himself as *Father, Son* and *Holy Spirit* is what we are to reflect, since we are made in the image of God. Let us consider each of these aspects of our Christian vocation:

God not only created the world, He *creates* it. Through the whole evolutionary process He has been engaged in the task of reducing chaos to order, as we read in the first part of Genesis. We are meant to be busy, within our particular limits and with the use of our unique and special talents, reducing chaos to order—in the physical world, in personal relationships. (How clever we are at doing the opposite—at reducing order to chaos, and how much more effectively can we do this these days, due to our scientific progress!) The late Lecomte du Noüy has pointed out that man is the first thing evolved which henceforth is in on the evolving. Due to the proliferation of God's creation and the elaborateness of His purposes the very individuality which marks our existence is valuable to Him in that each can do very special things *because* he is a tool fashioned in a unique way. This is true not only because of our gifts but because of confinement of those gifts: this is what so often gives a "cutting edge" to our abilities and actions.

God is busy redeeming men, meeting them where they are, taking up the hurt in their lives (as we have seen in Chapter IV). As we also saw there, we are meant to be busy as co-redeemers, sharing in the work of taking up the hurt in the lives of others, the work of meeting others where they are, of accepting the unacceptable so that in the protection of acceptance it may become more acceptable. Again our own limitations and inadequacies, even those which are represented by our sins, make us each unique and special helpmates of the redeeming God in meeting the needs of particular people around us.

God is Holy Spirit, that is (as we shall see in the next chapter), holy *esprit de corps*. And it is with us that He seeks to build the ideal community which is the Kingdom of God, namely, the inter-relationship in love of utterly unique people, each being fulfilled in terms of his own peculiar stamp.

Now we can sense, if not fully understand, the mystery of God's providence as it bears on our free will. God does not make evil, He does not will that we should be hurt. If we go beyond the evil, "beyond tragedy," in a sense of vocation, then the outcome can fulfill the will of God and fit in with His over-all design. And since He is the creative source of all the elements in any redeemed situation and is the source of the grace which enables us to transcend any confines of matter or spirit, then we rightly credit Him and His divine providence and can say as to all the good and fruitful activities of men, "Not unto us, not unto us, but unto thy name give the praise" (Ps. 115:1).

Now we are in a position to finish our analysis about what we do with our guilt. It is true that all that we do has abiding consequences. As Christians we confidently believe that God forgives our sins and that thereafter in our relations with Him there is no barrier between Him and us. In that sense our sins are done away with. But we are not the same persons after sin that we were before. In this sense, sins are not done away with. Sometimes our wrongdoing—our wrong choices, our injury to other persons—definitely closes doors to us, and limits the number of things that thereafter we may be able to do ourselves or work out with others. A man with a prison record may have been accepted as right by God because of his genuine repentance; he may even be accepted by family and friends. But he will probably not be accepted by a bonding company; and this in turn means that there are certain jobs that he can probably never hold, if he lives to be a hundred. No matter what *ought* to be the case, this will probably *be* the case. This is not only because of the hard-heartedness of men (though that is a serious factor to be taken into account); it is also because of a very reasonable caution on the part of people who have responsibilities for the interests of others—especially the proper caution of those in a fiduciary relationship. They might *personally* forgive and trust the other, but they cannot *officially* do so.

If limitations of which we are not the source can frustrate us, all the more can those limitations which are of our own making. But the answer is the same in either case. What is called for is a realistic analysis of where we are in life and what scope of activity is open to us and then the application of ourselves, with a sense of vocation, to produce the most fruitful results possible within the limitations. And here we can see the greatest miracle of grace; to be sure, past sin can hem us in, but it can also deepen us and intensify our effectiveness. The greater the sin, the greater can be the awareness of the grace of God, the more sensitively can we help others who are *in transitu* in their sins, the more genuine can be our sympathies, the more profound can be our humility.

This naturally gives rise to the question which St. Paul raises in passing, "Shall we sin the more that grace abound?" Of course, it is never good to sin. Those who know the reality of grace and want grace to abound will be the very ones who will not want to use this as an excuse for further sin. But once the sin is forgiven, then one can be even grateful for the sins themselves. So St. Augustine can exclaim, *"O felix*

*culpa!* O happy guilt, that brought so great a redemption"—
not only his own redemption, but through him the redemption of others. This point is lost by those who would "write
off," for example, a minister who had sinned conspicuously
before his ordination, or perhaps at some time during his ministry. They will say, "He shouldn't be a minister, because a
minister is supposed to be an example of what he preaches."
True. But the heart of what a Christian minister should be
preaching is the Gospel, that is, the good news of the forgiveness of sins. If the requirement for preaching were that one
be an example of the Sermon on the Mount, then we would
have no preachers. But many a minister's life presents a
living and inspiring example of belief in the forgiveness of
sins, the belief in God's judgment and God's grace, and of
the grateful response to forgiveness which expresses itself
in profound concern for others.

The same analysis applies no less to the deflections in our
path caused by the wrong of others. Many a young lady who
has been "let down" by someone she loved becomes, through
all her years, grateful that things worked out that way. In
the first place, we can resist the yearning that things had
worked out differently by the simple if rigorous logic that
compels us to admit that we have no way whatsoever of
knowing how things would have worked out had we *not* been
forced to take another road at some past time. We can specu-
late, but there is no way of providing factual foundation for
our speculations as to what another kind of future would
have been. In the second place—and this is the genuinely
religious answer—whether things would have been better or
not, *we are where we are,* and the task now is to get on with
the job—to fulfill our Christian vocation in terms of the here-
and-now situation and possibilities. The Christian Faith is
a realistic one. It does not avoid or remove tragedy, nor even
explain it very satisfyingly to our finite minds. But it does
provide the resources for living (to use Reinhold Niebuhr's

phrase) *"beyond tragedy."* Some who have known tragedy—resulting from causes hard to explain, from the wrongs of others, and especially from one's own false choices—and who have experienced the joy and fulfillment which comes from a sense of Christian vocation, have come to use as their favorite and most all-embracing prayer some form of words like those found in the Eucharist in the Anglican rite, *Here we offer and present unto thee, O Lord, our selves, our souls and bodies, to be a reasonable, holy, and living sacrifice unto thee. Reasonable,* that is, with a realistic appraisal of precisely what we have to offer here and now; *holy,* that is, dedicated in a sense of vocation—holy because of God's acceptance of us when we would dedicate ourselves to Him; *living,* that is, the active and vital use of ourselves, as limited, with the limitations now serving as channels of power, not just the "resigned" offering up to God of pains, hurts, and disappointments; *sacrifice,* that is, in recognition of the foundation fact that we belong to God from start to finish, and never simply to ourselves.

We said above that more power could come from the narrowed stream than from the broad river; but there was an *if*: if there is a turbine. This is the turbine: to rephrase it in terms of St. Paul's original injunction: "Present your bodies a living sacrifice, holy, acceptable unto God, which is your reasonable service" (Rom. 12:1). Since Jesus Christ is the supreme example of this very thing, the creedal answer to the problem of frustration is *He suffered under Pontius Pilate, was crucified* . . .

His followers are those who have followed Him to the Cross. They have known His peace, a peace that passes all understanding because it includes the paradox: "I came not to send peace, but a sword." One of His followers who knew suffering, William Alexander Percy, summed up his own

experience and that of the Apostles (and of many a Christian
in between) with these words:

> They cast their nets in Galilee
> Just off the hills of brown;
> Such happy, simple fisherfolk,
> Before the Lord came down.
>
> Contented, peaceful fishermen,
> Before they ever knew
> The peace of God that filled their hearts
> Brimful, and broke them too.
>
> Young John who trimmed the flapping sail,
> Homeless, in Patmos died.
> Peter, who hauled the teeming net,
> Head-down was crucified.
>
> The peace of God, it is no peace,
> But strife closed in the sod.
> Yet, brothers, pray for but one thing—
> The marvelous peace of God.

# Chapter VII

## *INDECISION*

Indecision is a sort of spiritual paralysis. It can incapacitate the best impulses. It can force solutions by default—which sometimes are fortuitous answers to problems, but which often are poorer answers than any of the choices under consideration.

The good side of indecision is the fact that it signalizes the finiteness of the human mind, the fallibility of human decision. In few important matters do we know enough of past, present or future really to know *for sure* what to do. Recognizing this fact is an important gain: it induces humility and also tolerance of those who reach opposite conclusions on the same facts; it also alerts us to maintain a continued critical attitude in the working out of solutions we may eventually adopt.

And as for those things where no action is called for, indecision is often the most suitable state of mind. Such is often the case with our assessment of other people: except where responsible action is at stake, "Judge not" is the best rule, and even when we must act, our necessary judgment should be a pragmatic one for the particular purpose only, not actually a judgment as to the real man—whom we do not know, and never can. And as to religious matters, there are many theological questions which can be asked—even interesting ones, for which the truest answer this side of the grave is "I don't know." Some religious groups quite properly regard a measure of agnosticism as a religious virtue.

But as to things which have a bearing on action—which can cover the whole range from the choice of religious and

70

ethical meanings, through evaluation of persons, to the calculation of physical risks—we must decide. Not to decide is
to decide. Not to decide is either to have others decide for
us, or to maintain the *status quo*—which is a decision for one
set of consequences as compared with another set. This is
true in big matters and little ones. If a man can't make up his
mind that God exists then he goes on living as though He
didn't, bereft of either His judgment or His grace. If a man
can't make up his mind to apply for a certain employment
opening, while he is wrestling with the matter, the opening
may be filled. If a man can't decide whether to walk home or
to take the last bus, his indecision will mean a decision to
walk if the bus pulls out while he meditates on the matter.
(Even the act of dalliance can have its own consequences:
an acquaintance who at a restaurant habitually spends five
minutes deciding between, say, a Spanish omelet and a veal
cutlet, is providing the data for others' estimate of his value-
pattern, especially if ever so often he changes his order in
midstream; and women spending too long in the decision
between two hats can irritate clerks, husbands and friends.)

Of course, in every one's life there are issues which because of their importance, their uniqueness, or their compli-
cation require careful, and perhaps sustained, study and
weighing. As to how to sort out such issues we will have
something to say later on. But if indecision is a more or less
consistent pattern in the life of an individual—if he is re-
peatedly in anguish over coming to conclusions, if he is constantly uneasy about decisions he has had finally to make,
the man is spiritually ill. The trouble is in the man, not in the
particular issues he is accustomed to face. What are the factors which make for an indecisive personality?

One is an *undisciplined imagination*. This is not a bad
thing but the abuse of a good thing. Man is much helped
in the process of deciding things by the fact that he can
project himself into the future and picture the situation

resulting from any given choice. Imagination has a further positive function. The image of a desirable outcome provides motive power to get a man off "dead center" and moving toward the outcome imagined. Thus, when a man does not get into action to grasp what seems to others an obvious opportunity, it is said of him, "He has no imagination." The imagination has also a negative, monitory function. We are able to picture the hazards which may lie in the particular course of action. This, of course, is very fortunate for two reasons. It may quite properly dissuade us from a given decision; or if that course of action still seems best, it enables us to anticipate all likely hazards and to shore up the situation against them. It is good to be ready for more ills than actually will befall us.

There seem to be virtually no limits to the range of the human imagination; and for this we can be grateful. But some people habitually apply to the least significant choice of steps ahead a range of imagination which would match that of a writer of detective stories or of science fiction. Every possible contingency is conjured up; every possible twist in the motives of others is visualized; every type of conspiracy between the people involved is taken into account; every possible failure of physical resources is pictured —and then all of this is lived through in advance until one is literally terrified at the prospect. If the same imaginative fantasy is indulged in as to the other alternative open, then the decider is literally "stymied." Fearful to move either direction, one or the other (or a third possibility) is decided by default. Or if he finally brings himself to a positive decision, he sets upon the road robbed of the joy of the adventure by the sense of being surrounded by so many perils. Or the opposite can happen. Men of a more optimistic make-up can so expand upon the rich possibilities of any direction of life that they render it almost impossible to choose.

Now the fault here is not with the imagination, nor even with the fertility of it. But what we need in addition to imagination—as a companion to imagination—is a *discrimination* which can sort out from the things imagined those factors which are probable from those which are merely possible, and of the latter, those that are merely fantastic—that is, virtually impossible except by a "fluke." As the images developed by conscious reflection (or in a somewhat uninhibited way by the unconscious mind) pass in review, a stern censor should be standing by to evaluate, preserve and discard the images. In other words, imagination, like every other good aspect of human life, must be under discipline. But we would be helped in the exercise of such discipline if we were free from certain false suppositions which tend to persuade us to hold on to every figment of our imaginations. These false notions are:

(1) Given enough thought, a solution can be reached in which one gains all the advantages and suffers no disadvantages.

(2) There is one right answer to every human problem.

(3) By no means must a mistake be made.

To unearth these notions that are so often implicit in our thinking, and to state them in black and white, is almost enough to refute them. But just a word about each:

(1) You can't have everything. In the finite world every course of action involves limited possibilities. The very act of taking a course of action means excluding possibilities. To use the familiar "mountain vs. beach" vacation problem, if you decide for the shore, you simply can't have the bracing mountain air or the inspiration of great woods; if you go to the mountains you simply won't have use for your surfboard nor can you enjoy the tang of salt air. We are usually clever enough to recognize these realities when it comes to something so tangible as a vacation spot; we are often not so realistic in the decision to get married or in the choice of a job. To have some things means the giving up of other

things. A man would rarely deny himself and his family a vacation by saying stubbornly on one day, "I simply won't go to Sea Breeze Beach because I can't climb mountains there," and on the next day, "I would be miserable at Pine Glade because I love the salt water"—but we quite often act precisely this way in much more important matters.

(2) Only if a man had the mind of God could he talk relevantly about "*the* right answer" to a complex problem. We cannot "go off in all directions at once" and so must choose the direction we would go; but often at a crossroads we are presented with genuinely rich possibilities of a number of the roads which lie out before us, if we travel the road set upon with continued energy and imagination. The romantic fallacy that there is only "one true love" can breed an indecision which may leave the believer a bachelor or a spinster. This is an open universe, not a closed, mechanical one. What is right and best is something being formed creatively as life moves on. Any "predestination" that there is takes all this into account. God's foreknowledge takes into account the free creative possibilities. Being neither blessed nor burdened with foreknowledge ourselves, we especially must be open to them.

(3) This same thing applies to decisions which can even be recognized along the way as outright mistakes. God's grace and flexibility are such and man's possibilities are such that even mistaken situations can be redeemed and great results follow. We have already discussed this in the last chapter and seen that the point may even be reached when we are grateful for our mistakes—even for our sins. But it is mentioned again here because fear of making a mistake can be a paralyzing factor of the first order. In important matters careful thought and calculation of risk are, of course, called for; but even in important matters the healthy mind will include a dash of carelessness, which is ultimately grounded in religious faith. Needed is a sense of confidence and spontaneity which frees us for action when the time comes for

action. We can have this if we are undergirded with the trust that God has yet more wonders to perform, that even beyond our wrong choices, He awaits us to carry on with us. This is the trust that in the realm of personal life there are really no dead-end streets from which we cannot at least cut across to a better road or retrace our steps back to a junction (but we rarely really do the latter because the geographical analogy breaks down here: in addition to space there is time —the map is changing as well as the people). If we have burned our bridges, there are always open to us other ways to travel if we are traveling with God. This conviction frees us to take risks, though, to be sure, they should be calculated risks. This should also free us from taking ourselves too seriously, or being too sober about life. All does not hang on the outcome of any of our decisions.

There is a further factor which makes for an indecisive personality, and one which by and large is the most important one. It is *lack of clarity as to the objectives of life.* We need not dwell on this point here because it was the central theme of the second chapter (on "Fear"). If a man does not know what he wants most from life he is in a poor way to get it. For decisive action we need to be clear as to our priority scale of values. As we have seen, nothing else can completely and consistently order man's life than to have God and His will the absolutely first thing and all other aims subordinated to Him. Mixed motives dominating in life lead to mixed reactions at the moments of decision. Purity of heart, Kierkegaard has reminded us, is to will one thing. The *scope* of the problem of decision is very much narrower when the question "What do I want to do?" has been translated into "What is the will of God?" This leads us then directly to the question which was left open in the last chapter: "How can we know the will of God?"

Half of the truth is stated when we simply answer "We can't!" Of course, there are many simple and obvious matters of conduct in which we can act with virtual certainty. But for the kinds of questions that create the indecision which we are here considering (where a genuine doubt is set up in our minds), we dare not—without some qualifications—identify the conclusion we reach with the will of God. Know as much as we can, weigh as we will, we never know everything about a situation and we are never quite accurate in our evaluation of the respective factors. God alone sees all and weighs aright. The best that we can hope to do is to be clear about our objectives, as pure as possible in our motivations, as well informed as possible about our facts, and as balanced as possible about our judgments—all of which adds up to saying that we must act according to what we *hope* is the will of God. God does not expect infallibility of us, nor should we expect it of ourselves—or of other men.

God has not provided us with the means of being any more sure. He could, of course, supply us with direct instructions for each difficult situation—perhaps by a direct word, or by some confirming sign at the conclusion of our deliberations. As Jesus pointed out, men seek a sign. But He tells us that we shall have no sign.

There are two ways to build a house. One is to engage a carpenter and to stand over him and tell how to cut each board, where to place the nails, etc., and repeat the same process with plumber, painter, roofer, and so on. The other way is to engage a contractor, give him a rough sketch of what one wants, provide him with the means to get the materials, and tell him to go ahead and build the house. The latter is risky in some ways; but it is the way that God deals with us in our discharge of life. This may be risky, too—human history certainly shows that it is. But it is what gives dignity to human life. Returning to the illustration, most men of competence and self-respect would rather be the contractor than the carpenter over whom the builder stood hour after hour. To change the figure, we are God's field agents, or branch managers, with much discretion in carrying out the general policies of the firm in the particular area put in our charge. Those familiar with the workings of the Federal Government will recognize that there is a much more personal fulfillment in working for an agency which is charged with the fulfillment of a responsible task and which affords a wide range of discretion in the discharge of it— such as the State Department or the Securities and Exchange Commission—as compared with working in an agency in which every possible contingency is covered by rule and regulation, such as the Post Office Department or the Civil Service Commission. There is much less danger of error and corruption in the latter, but there is generally much more opportunity for personal fulfillment in the former. And men not working by a punch-clock, in fact, generally put in more hours, and more fruitful ones, than those who do. Much as we yearn for a sign at crucial points of indecision, we should be grateful that God has chosen another way with us. This is simply part of the fact that God is more interested in us than in our conduct. He at least is not afflicted with the modern mentality that wants only to "get results." He wants us to grow in grace and be mature companions in His creative, redemptive, and community-building work. We must do the deciding, but He has not left us totally without aids in the decision. We shall now consider what resources are available to us as we seek to know the will of God and some of the steps that we should take in making serious decisions.

1. *The general will of God for man.* Some people pray only when they are in serious difficulty and it is a commonplace that, though such prayers are often effective and comforting, it is better to be praying all along. The same is true of seeking the will of God. We should not ponder this matter only when a crisis comes. We should take our religion seriously enough that we are always giving thought to God's general purposes with men. We are most apt to do His will in particular things if we have identified our will with His

will and are *for* what He is for, day in and day out.

This is not a mere sentiment. It means conscious study and attention to the Christian Faith, to the Christian interpretation of history, to the Christian understanding of man, to the scheme of Christian ethics. If we have joined our purposes with God's in action, concern and prayer, over the days and years, particular problems do not represent so much of a crisis, nor do we have to seek to muster our spiritual resources at a time when it is usually most difficult to do so.

2. *Purity of motivation.* In dealing with a particular problem, *why* we may be inclined toward one solution or the other does not of itself determine the right answer. We are not always supposed to choose the thing that is most personally painful to us or that which we would enjoy the least. There are some people who err in this direction: with a submerged martyr complex, they somehow feel more righteous in choosing a non-attractive course of action. A curious perversion of this approach, which is, in fact, its opposite, is to dress up—by rationalization—a desire as a sacrifice. "I really would not have wanted to spend that much money for an electric train, but, of course, it has meant a great deal to my boy." "*I* would have been perfectly happy to have my wife's mother live with us, but I felt that my wife had to be protected from that sort of imposition." "I would have been perfectly happy to give my assistant another chance after he blew up at me, but I think it's better for *him* to learn a lesson; so I fired him." While it does not give us the answer to know what our motives are, it often clarifies the situation and removes from the picture unworthy motives—ones which could not suffer the light of day.

People who have made a habit of rationalization are not very sensitive to their own motives in connection with particular choices; so here again the general habit of our lives plays a large part in the conclusions we come to in particular cases. That is why the practice of the regular examination of conscience (provided it is accompanied with a lively faith in God's abundant accepting power, which enables us to dare to face ourselves honestly, with the knowledge that we can accept ourselves even when we have seen what we really are) can get us out of the ruts of rationalization and can make us accustomed to putting questions on their right footing. As we have seen in Chapter IV, examination of conscience has to do not only with clearing up the past, but clearing the road ahead as well. Purity of heart is something that needs constant cultivation: it is not something that we produce for a particular occasion. A familiar prayer bids us not to "begin an action without a pure intention." Without this element, we are apt to miss the mark in any attempt to do the will of God.

3. *Personal experience.* Regular examination of conscience not only helps us to clarify our motives, it affords a reflective summary of our experience. It helps us utilize it as a resource in future decisions. But personal experience is not only a negative factor. It is really a misleading consolation for a mistake when a man says, "Well, it has taught me a lesson." Had he made the right decision, it would have taught him a lesson also—if he were accustomed to reflect on each day's activities.

Personal experience must be used with a caution. We cannot generalize too readily on a given experience. Life is always in flux; we are never the same people that we were, and those with whom we deal are not just units, they are unique people. So we should beware of pat answers or sets of mind which express themselves in such words as, "I *always* do thus and so."

4. *General experience.* This caution applies also in the application of adages and platitudes to particular situations. One of the glories of the way in which God has arranged

human life is the utter uniqueness of each moment in the life of each person, not to mention the utter uniqueness of each person with whom we have to do. A rich vicarious sharing in the experiences of others, a familiarity with literature (which often provides us with a wide range of such experience, and this is especially so of the Bible), can extend the range of one's imagination and alert him to opportunities and dangers in many types of situation. But again we must not forget the special character of every situation. A recognition of this fact is one of the most fruitful rewards of reading the Bible. Here we find not so much general rules for action as a display of the factors at work in the lives of men who in a covenant relationship with God worked out their lives under His judgments and dedicated to His service. The applications there are as manifold as life is manifold, yet the common factors at work are as relevant today as they were in Biblical times: a sense of vocation under God; His searching judgments; the workings of grace; redemption beyond sin, frustration and mistake.

5. *The principles of Christian ethics.* Some might feel that this heading should be No. 1; but the kinds of questions we are concerned with here are those which by definition do not admit of ready answers. There is no answer in the books for a man who wants to know if it is right for him to leave the advertising business and study medicine; whether he ought to marry Anne or Sue—or at all; or whether he and his wife should adopt a baby. Obviously, all conduct comes under the two great Commandments (love of God with one's whole strength and love of one's neighbor as oneself). But in situations like this, there is often a conflict of claims of "neighbors"; and as to the love of God, the very question at stake is which particular use of time, talents, energy or money is the best use of it for God.

Apart from the two great Commandments, Christian ethical principles fall into two categories: explicit rules covering given areas of conduct, and principles of priority between claims. We should consider separately the bearing of each of these types of principles in the problem of deciding what the will of God is in a particular matter.

Particular rules of ethics, such as the Ten Commandments, represent the experience of the people of the Covenant (that is, the Old and New Israel) seeking to order human behavior, and in this seeking guided by the Holy Spirit Who dwells with the community. Our own personal experience (conditioned, to be sure, by this very community) validates these norms and usually the Christian will not question them. If a man is in doubt as to whether to pocket ten dollars he finds in a lost wallet, he needs only to remind himself of the Commandment "Thou shalt not steal." If he is very angry at one who has insulted him and he happens to have a pistol handy, he will, we hope, simply recall the Commandment "Thou shalt do no murder." If he is tempted to play golf on Sunday morning rather than to go to church, his situation is covered at least analogically by "Remember that thou keep holy the Sabbath-day."

But there is a higher law than even these Commandments, a law on which hangs "all the Law and the Prophets"; and in the endeavor to fulfill God's will in a particular instance, a man may in some situations have to bring the higher law to bear upon the lower. If his children are starving and he knows that the owner of the wallet is a man of means, it may very well be his duty (granting certain circumstances which we need not spell out here) to buy bread and milk and eggs with the ten dollars. If he is in military service, the circumstances of the particular war may be such that he must kill the enemy within his area of fire—though this appears to violate the sixth Commandment. If his wife is ill on a Sunday morning and he should take her to the hospital, these are circumstances in which it would be the will of God that he not go to church. Workers in the French underground during the last war felt that lying, homicide, and adultery were part of moral duty in the exercise of their task of helping save the nation; and the Christian conscience has ratified their actions. (An instructive example from sacred literature is the betrayal of the Assyrian commander by Judith, who after a magnificent prayer to God, and well equipped with finery and lies, went forth to the camp and attracted Holofernes with her charms; and though she apparently was prepared to spend the night with him, her honor was saved by the fact that since he had drunk more than she had, she had the opportunity to cut off his head with his own sword.)

These more dramatic examples, though they do not parallel the more usual problems with which we are apt to be faced, illustrate the fact that even the most time-honored items in the Judaeo-Christian code of ethics are subject to review by the two great Commandments. An ethical decision is rather simple when the question is simply "Shall I kill this man whom I don't like?" There we don't have to think back to the two great Commandments and weigh and balance; we can simply apply the Commandment about murder. But when the question is "What can I do to keep my nation from being destroyed?" the question is more complicated. Weighing all things up, there are circumstances in which the ethical answer might be pacifism; but an absolute pacifism, however reassuring the simplicity of the solution may be, overlooks one set of claims in the recognition of another set. Another oversimplification would be the application of the normal rules of honesty to a prisoner who is being interrogated by his captors about the location of his compatriots. We honor Judith more for her deceit and her highly suggestive behavior than we would honor her, under the circumstances, for candor and modesty that would normally be more becoming.

But this must be said: the presumption is on the side of established moral law. The case for violating it must be a very strong one, or one can be misled very easily by a mixture of motives. Though a careful sorting out of one's motives is always important, it is especially so whenever we feel called upon to make ourselves an exception to established moral law. All the other norms for seeking the will of God should give a pretty clear "green light" before we place on our consciences the burden of violating one of the Commandments or the generally received applications of them which have behind them the weight of the experience of the whole people of God. We should be particularly wary in making an exception which happens to bring us personal benefit or save us from personal hurt.

Those portions of the Christian Church which place a high evaluation upon individual moral responsibility under the direct judgment of God do not have as a part of their tradition a detailed code of ethics covering every contingency. But they do supply us with the principles of decision (of the type that we have been considering) and with guidance as to the priorities to be applied.

Rather basic, for example, is the order of claims in family problems. "Therefore shall a man leave his father and his mother, and shall cleave unto his wife . . ." puts the integrity and safeguarding of the marriage relationship above loyalties to others. In general the priority scale would be: spouse, children, parents, brothers and sisters, other relatives. Obviously, there is nothing absolute about such a scheme, and no automatic answers are provided. For example, one should not buy a new coat for one's daughter (even though the old one is worn) with the only money available to keep one's mother from starving. But suppose a wife has found over the years that her husband and her mother do not get on well, and upon the death of her father her mother wants very much to move in. If means are available to find some other solution (though it may not be one as desirable in the mother's eyes), concern for her spouse's happiness and their mutual harmony would outweigh the wishes of even her own mother. Likewise, every claim of the children for time and attention (though each particular occasion might be beneficial to them) does not outweigh the important factor of some opportunity for the couple themselves to enjoy each other—alone. And one cannot dissipate funds needed as a minimal base for one's children's education even in what would otherwise be quiet proper assistance to various relatives in their difficulties.

The approach to matters like this is, first, to recognize all valid claims upon us; second, assess our means; third, search the purity of our motivations; and, fourth, apply the established priority scale. Then, there is a further duty: since we're dealing here not with blacks and whites but with claims of various intensity, we must seek to find ways to meet, as far as we can, the claims which we had to give second place. A positive duty of providing personal companionship for the mother in the illustration, as well as attempting to induce co-operation in this regard from the husband, who is being given first place; attempts to find other means of support or of self-help for the relatives rejected in the other illustration—are samples of ethical corollaries which arise after the initial decision has been made. Our motivation for the exercise of these further duties will be strengthened if we recognize in such situations—as in all—that we are never certain enough of our decisions nor sufficiently free from a mixture of motives to be self-righteous about a firm adherence to the decision made. And it is the positive duty of each of us to so dispose our affections and concerns, whenever possible, that we avoid putting burdens on the consciences of others which will force upon them the application of priority scales. Nothing can help produce harmony in a marriage more than for a son-in-law and daughter-in-law to take the initiative in acting on behalf of a spouse's parents.

6. *Advice and counsel.* It is almost too obvious to say that in difficult questions we should check our insights with other people. But the important question is, What other peo-

ple? Friends and acquaintances who may be estimable in many ways can be very unsuitable as counselors. The greatest danger is the person who habitually senses what we *want* to do and encourages that course of action. This type of response to a request for help sometimes arises out of a desire to be agreeable, but often it actually represents a diffidence to the concern at hand. It is easier to say, "If that's what you want to do, you ought to go right ahead" or, "You're absolutely right; that's just how I would feel myself" than to provide careful and discriminating analysis of the motivations and the consequences of proposed action. On the other hand, if in the counselor a proper courage as to convictions passes over into a desire to dominate and blueprint the lives of others, we are in equal danger, especially if the other's method of domination is a subtle one. What we should want from a counselor is not an answer but *help*—honest and concerned—in sorting out the issues and in the evaluation of the various factors involved.

The mention of evaluation points to another important ingredient. All evaluation stems from the ethical outlook—and back of that, the whole world-view—of the evaluator. For example, a person who genially regards all religious differences as unimportant (on the implicit or explicit assumption that none of it is true) is perhaps not the best person to advise a Protestant young lady as to whether she should promise, as a condition of marriage, that her children be raised Roman Catholics. Nor is a person whose philosophy is a sort of prudential hedonism the best advisor to a Christian who is trying to decide his life vocation. Nor is a person who takes a purely relativistic view of sex ethics perhaps the most useful person to advise a young lady who has not adopted this view of things, on the proper degree of expression of affection to her fiancé. We should choose our advisors from among those who will make their analysis of our particular problem from the standpoint of the world-view which we feel is the sound one and by which we have decided to live.

No counseling is truly objective. This applies to professional counselors (including psychologists and psychotherapists) no less than to lay folk. The very way one defines the issues, the very questions one asks, the very emphasis one puts on one aspect of the data as contrasted with another aspect—all this is affected by one's outlook. And the situation is not altered substantially even if one professes to engage in "non-directive counseling." But if the best professional consultant available is one with a different worldview than our own, then we should take this fact into account in evaluating his diagnosis, and if we are inclined to accept his view of the matter on this level (which well might be the case), we must still be wary of his conclusions and recommendations. A few years ago a prominent psychoanalyst traced a business executive's emotional disturbances to his wife (and, under the circumstances, there was much to be said for this conclusion). Then he recommended, "Why don't you divorce her and marry a woman of a different type? That's what I did, and now I'm fine." Fortunately, the patient—though a secularist himself—recoiled from this approach. Since then, both husband and wife have had the benefit of a significant religious re-orientation, the husband is well, and the two apparently are getting along quite satisfactorily. This is an extreme case (and, we may assume, a quite unusual professional prescription); but it highlights the importance, even for more ordinary situations, of the counselor's religious and ethical perspective.

Experience is obviously an important part of the desirable equipment for those to whom we go for help. But it is important that the proposed counselor has himself reacted constructively to his experience and has achieved mature, wholesome solutions. If this is not the case, cynicism and moral nihilism may color the advice. Wives who are not getting on with their husbands are sometimes tempted to "weep on the shoulder" of others who seem to be in the same fix—especially where the existence of the common problem has been signalized by drastic solutions like divorce or separation. Of course, it is emotionally satisfactory to receive comfort from those who have or have had the same problems, but the price of receiving such comfort is often a subtle distortion of the outlook of the counselee and the underlining of the destructive tendencies in his reaction to the problem at hand.

Finally, we should be careful to choose advisors whom we can trust to keep our confidences. A warning is found in the story of the four ministers in a small town who decided to confide in each other their principal faults in order to receive help in correcting them. One man confessed that he was addicted to the bottle and from time to time went down to the city for a two- or three-day "binge"; another confessed that he was something of a kleptomaniac regarding the alms; the third confessed that he was a gambler and had gotten in deep with gambling debts; the fourth hesitated to mention his fault—but when pressed admitted, "My worst fault is gossip—and I can hardly wait to get out of here!" Quite seriously, there are very few people (apart from those who serve as counselors in a professional way) who can be trusted to be totally discreet about the affairs of another. And some problems are of such a nature that widespread knowledge of one or another of the personal factors involved only complicates the solution of the problem. Even if the subject matter of the problem is not one which need be kept secret, the very fact that a number of people have come to know about the matter adds to the self-consciousness of the person making his deliberations and adds to the pressures toward one or another of the solutions—especially toward the solutions that other people have already decided are the best.

For a Christian who seeks to achieve solutions which approximate the will of God, the fullest combination of all these counseling qualifications is likely to be found in a priest or minister in one's own religious tradition. The frame of reference for his analysis and recommendations will be the same as that to which the counselee has committed himself. He is likely to have had a wide experience—both personal and vicarious; and he will have seen many problems through to their conclusion—having seen constructive and redeeming outcomes as well as destructive and frustrating ones. Both by training and because of the nature of his position, he is less likely to be a "yes-man" on the one hand or a dominator of lives on the other. In other words, he is likely to be *interested* and *disinterested*—each in the proper sense. And by moral commitment and long-standing habit he will doubtless be one who knows how to keep his ears open and his mouth shut. He is "under the seal"—which people tend to associate with the confessional, but which is equally the recognized responsibility of the parson in any tradition.

Speaking of confession, it is fortunate that more attention is being given to this aspect of the ministry these days. Tied up with our indecision as to the future is often a burden of guilt from the past. We are often pushed into solutions which are unwise by the guilt we feel for the mistakes we have already made, especially when these have adversely affected other people. Or, if we have not understood the nature of our past wrongs and the motivations which brought them about, we may get a distorted picture of what is the best way to "make up" for them or to create a better situation. The "lay of the land" as to tomorrow's action has been very much shaped by what we did yesterday and what we are today as a result. A priest or minister can serve a double function here; through his experience and knowledge of moral theology he can help us understand those things which make us feel guilty, help us sort out what was, in fact, guilt and what was, in fact, not. And, second, acting in the name of God and of the Christian fellowship, he can assure us that we can start fresh, thus freeing us from the dead weight of guilt from the past which so often distorts the present and future and thus releasing us (literally the meaning of "absolution") to see with more clarity what restitution or amends are possible or appropriate and what the new shape of our lives should be.

A recognition of, and release from, a sense of guilt quite often is a stimulus to making amends; on the other hand, a sense of forgiveness by God will often free us from the compulsion to "make up" for the past in ways that are in fact unwise and can do more harm than good. A woman who, after divorcing her husband, came to the realization that her faults were much greater than his and that she had wronged him deeply, decided that she should make contact with her husband, tell him how wrong she was, and not only seek his forgiveness but establish a relationship as "friends." Normally this would seem very commendable, except that meanwhile he had married again and was off to a good start building a new life. It happened that her approach was responded to all too well and both she and her husband were projected into emotional complications which almost resulted in two wrecked marriages instead of one. Naturally, one would suspect a mixture of motives in her attempt to remedy things, but if in the context of counsel and confession she could have been freed of the sense of guilt about the past, then the element of selfish desire which may have been involved would at least have been left isolated and she would have been faced with the real nature of her efforts at the renewal of friendly relations.

On the other hand, in the relationship of past guilt to proper future action, in order to relieve ourselves from painful responsibilities we often too readily "clear ourselves" or minimize our own part in the distress that has come to others. If we have caused financial loss to someone, we tend to say, "He was in a better position to lose it than I was," or "Well, he acted with his eyes open," or other variants of "I am not my brother's keeper." The counselor who acts as moral theologian as well as prudential advisor can often help us see the real nature of our conduct and confront us with the necessity for genuine repentance and an intention to make real restitution. Whether by retaining the weight of our sins or by sloughing them off we are distorting our vision of our future responsibilities, we may well profit from the help of one who has been charged with the function Christ entrusted to him in the words, "Whose sins thou dost forgive, they are forgiven; whose sins thou dost retain, they are retained."

7. *Prayer and "guidance."* Ultimately, of course, one must take the responsibility himself for the decision he finally reaches. In the throes of indecision, people are often so fearful to do this very thing that they find talking to other people—often quite widely—much easier on them than quietly facing the matter themselves. This they must finally do. The best context for this quite necessary exercise is that of prayer. In turning one's thoughts upward and in analyzing the situation under the eye of the Almighty, things will be seen in better proportion. In the forum of prayer our unworthy motivations stand condemned and we recognize that we must reject them. That in us which tends to sacrifice for others and give full place to their needs is nourished. Our confidence that all does not depend upon our decision in the particular case and our trust in resources beyond even our own mistakes, is magnified.

So much for our side of the matter. But Christians also believe that prayer is a two-way communication. We do believe that in prayer God's Holy Spirit really does (to adapt phrases of familiar prayers) "purify our consciences," "cleanse the thoughts of our hearts," help us toward "a right judgment in all things," "defend us from error," "lead us into truth," "save us from false choices," and "enlighten and strengthen us for God's service." This is all in a way that does not deny our freedom or make automatons out of us. Generally our guidance does not come in terms of black-and-white answers but in terms of the compunction of conscience, clarification of issues, alertness to inconspicuous but important factors in the case, strength to follow the leadings of conscience, and the warming of our hearts to help us *want* to do the will of God once discerned.

Is there such a thing as "guidance" in terms of precise answers? The testimony of holy men of heart, and the occasional experience—at least a few times in a life-time—of even garden-variety Christians, is such that we cannot ignore the real possibility of insights so direct and so clear, or exterior phenomena so striking, that they represent direct word from on high in answer to a personal problem. But this is not normally God's way of dealing with us and to assume that it is (as have various cults from time to time) is to court three dangers.

First, this approach often cultivates in its devotees an inattention to the hard work of thought, investigation and counsel, "groaning and travail" which is a necessary part of a life of sound action and which deepens us in our spiritual maturity and in our sympathy for the problems of others. To expand an old formula: we should think and work as though all depended upon ourselves and pray as though all depended upon God. The former is as important as the latter.

Second, what we take for the Holy Spirit may sometimes be the devil. Which, at the least, is a way of saying that the contents of our unconscious minds are so complicated, and our conscious minds are so devious in rationalizing unconscious urges that we dare not presume to attribute to God all that pushes itself to the fore in our minds. We must, as St. Paul advised, "distinguish between spirits." We should be particularly suspicious of guidance which coincides too nearly with our self-interest or with what we wanted to do before we started to pray or which does not "check out" with other tests and aids of the types considered above.

Third, those who make a pattern of acting on "direct guidance" often display a dogmatism about their conclusions, an impatience of opposition, which are undesirable traits of personality—and would be even if the "guided" person were right ninety per cent of the time. Even if we are pretty sure that our conclusions are "inspired," we should be reticent about imposing them upon other people—even supposedly for their own good, especially when the conclusions appear to be obviously for our good. At a meeting of a "spiritual uplift" group in Washington a few years back, the lady chairman proposed the holding of a large banquet at an expensive hotel for "a spiritual witness to the Nation's Capitol." She suggested "a quiet time." When it was over, she said it had come to her clearly that Mr. —— should be the treasurer of the project. When it came the turn of the gentleman's wife to reveal her "guidance" the group got a somewhat schizoid impression of the Holy Ghost, for she reported that it had come to her that her husband should quite definitely not be the treasurer!

8. *What we want to do.*   Our repeated strictures against self-serving decisions, particularly when they are masked as altruistic ones, might give the impression that we are safe in deciding for what we don't want to do, for what seems the unpleasant course of action. Such a rule would certainly rob us of the "joy in the life that now is" for which we pray, and would imply that we are to remain permanently torn personalities, robbed of the "abundant life" which Christ promised His followers.

In the field of vocational choice, for example, that a man wants to do a particular thing is an important plus factor in the direction of that particular calling. Obviously, when a man enjoys working with things much more than dealing with people, he will serve God better as a mechanic than as a sales manager. That a man *wants* to marry a particular young lady is an important—indeed essential—ingredient in a decision to marry her. In estimating the chances for success in either a vocation or a marriage, a burning desire is an important motivation for loyalty and perseverance. When we have a freedom of choice (taking all our responsibilities and commitments into account), that a particular thing "just comes natural" is a strong clue to the way in which God would have us serve Him. This is not only because we will do a better job of it that way, but also one of the ends of creation is the joy of our days.

*Why* we most enjoy a particular way is worth inspecting. Hell can be defined as getting what we wanted when we wanted the wrong things (there is a story about a priest in Hell submerged in mud up to his neck who claimed that he was happy because he was standing on the Bishop's head). A dedicated minister who turned down a most attractive call was asked if he hadn't really wanted to take it. He said, "Very much—but for all the wrong reasons." So often there are conflicts between what we very much want and what all indications tell us that we should want. If the latter really wins it is also because of a natural want—it is because we come to desire something even more than what we can identify separately as our own desires. It means we really want to do the will of God. The degree to which this one desire can dominate all other desires is the degree to which we can do the will of God and enjoy life at the same time. (This brings us back again to the end of Chapter IV, where we were discussing what the grateful love of God could do to our personalities.)

But such is not a result we can count on on a "short-order" basis. This full answer to indecision comes with a regular life of prayer, with regular self-examination, that "having the eyes of the mind opened to behold things invisible and unseen, we may in heart be inspired by God's wisdom, and in work be upheld by his strength, in the end be accepted of him as his faithful servants."

There is another fruit of consistency in devotion to the will of God and application to the means of the union of our wills with His: we can be saved from the indecision which can follow our decisions. Lot's wife, who in looking back to Sodom turned to a pillar of salt, stands as a symbol of the way we can be frozen in our tracks by a sort of irrational fear that we have made a wrong decision or one that called for us to give up too much. There are times when we must reconsider, must retrace our steps. But when we have given a matter every possible consideration and life has moved on, we are hampered in effective action by a sort of lingering uneasiness. A steady trust in God will relieve us of this burden, because we know that He abides with us no less in our steps on a new path than He did at the crossroads. The continuity of God's presence and our trust that He will continue to prompt us and support us through His Spirit are expressed in this ancient Christian prayer, which well might form part of our personal prayers—not only in moments of crisis but as we pursue the tasks we have undertaken:

> Direct us, O Lord, in all our doings, with thy most gracious favour, and further us with thy continual help; that in all our works begun, continued, and ended in thee, we may glorify thy holy Name, and finally, by thy mercy, obtain everlasting life; through Jesus Christ our Lord.

# Chapter VIII

## *LONELINESS*

THAT UNIVERSAL EMOTION known as loneliness tells us two important things about ourselves. One meaning points inward, one outward. Our loneliness is a reflection of the fact that each man knows that no other person can share the secret of his inner self. It is also a reflection of the fact that we are not whole of ourselves: our lives must be interlaced with others if we are to be fulfilled.

Thus what we have said of fear is true of loneliness. It is a good thing—if consciously understood—because it tells us the truth about ourselves. Its pangs can then lead us to establish the relationships which will complete us—inwardly and outwardly.

In a day when there is much talk about individualism, sociology and social psychology have nevertheless sufficiently come to the center of the intellectual stage that popular works dealing with the happiness of the individual tend to develop their solutions almost exclusively in terms of inter-personal relations. In other words, the problem is conceived as how to make introverts more extrovert. Granted that life and personality should be shared, the primary question still remains: how to have a life and personality worth sharing. Persons need to grow in depth as well as in width. And a good part of the problem in our culture is to help extroverts develop more inwardness. Of course, the grand hypothesis on which the other approach rests is that man is a socially-conditioned animal, with no other frame of reference for his meaning than the social milieu. But the Biblical view of man sees him placed at the intersection of two lines: his fulfillment depends upon his right orientation toward God (which is ultimately an inward relationship) and neighbor (which rests on outgoingness). The two great commandments, then, are not simply two laws of conduct; they are descriptions of man aplomb.

Corresponding to these two dimensions of our fulfillment are two yearnings: one is the desire to have close relations with people; the other is the desire to withdraw from people and to be alone. The degree to which these two press upon one varies as widely as do people. But in most of us there is something of the companion and something of the hermit. Frustration of the first in us we call loneliness. Actually frustration of the second is really loneliness too, as we shall see a little later on. But since the former is the more easily recognized, we shall turn to it first.

On a subway a maximum number of people are crowded into a minimum amount of space. Yet nothing can be more of a setting for loneliness than a subway ride. It is a burlesque of human unrelatedness. We have an optimum opportunity to study the faces of other people (there's nothing else to do—it's too noisy to meditate; and one can hardly be accused of staring—there is a limited number of directions to look); yet we have absolutely no access to what these faces represent. The very propinquity emphasizes our almost complete atomization. Whether the resulting emotion of loneliness is mild or acute will depend upon whether with the individual the experience is a transitory one or is a symbol of the normal situation. In any case it affords us a clue to what loneliness is: it is not coterminous with "being alone"; it is *unrelatedness*.

But we have to be more precise than that; there is no

such thing as total unrelatedness. Even in the subway there are at least two kinds of relationship: the passengers are all members of the human race, and, temporarily at least, they are all going in the same direction. But the connection between me and the person to my right lacks two things: it is transitory and it is on a superficial basis. Both play their part. In the club car of a train two people may "hit it off" and may virtually bare their souls to one another, but the knowledge that their paths will probably never cross again may make the experience one which deepens the sense of loneliness in the participants. On the other hand, a man may see the same people year in and year out, but they may be no assuagement to his loneliness, because the level of relatedness is not profound enough. Thus, insofar as it has to do with interpersonal relations, we may define loneliness as the lack of *deep* and *abiding* connections with people.

Conversation is not the sole measure of personal relationship, but it is fairly indicative. What would a tape-recording of the average social gathering reveal by way of the depth of personal interconnections?

"Well, Mrs. White, how are you?" (To which the answer will probably be "Fine," regardless of the diagnostic situation, since in any case the questioner doubtless doesn't care; or perhaps the answer will be skipped entirely, the question merely being repeated, with emphasis now on the last word.) "Where are you living now? In Jersey, you say? Well, it's nice over there; good to be out of the city. We have a place up in Yonkers—convenient for my husband's work, you know. Did I hear you say that you will be summering in Maine? My sister and her husband go to Maine. The distances are so great there you probably wouldn't know them. Have you tried these hors d'oeuvres? Oh, there's someone just coming in I want to speak to; but before I leave you, I want you to know my friend, Mrs. Livingstone. You two ought to get acquainted: she lives in Jersey, too. Well, we must get together sometime; my very best to your husband."

Now this may be a great deal better than saying nothing; and there are times when in fact we have no more than this to say. But if the bulk of our hours with others are spent on the general level of which the above is a parody, then we are bound to be lonely—consciously or unconsciously.

What of conversation about more serious subjects? Perhaps such talk will be more worth while, broadening our outlook and store of information. But of itself it does not bring people closer together. We participate in many a discussion in which there has been much airing of views, when actually we can't remember, a day later, the names of those taking part. Of course, serious levels of discourse provide an *opportunity* for us to know the make-up of other individuals. But so does "small talk," in a measure. Whether this opportunity is realized in genuine personal connections depends upon *personal involvement*. What provides this?

Common concerns usually serve better than common talk. Partners in a business enterprise may come to know each other intimately, their affiliation on the personal level nourished by the sharing of hopes and fears, the rejoicing in success and the commiserating in failures. So with collaboration in causes which transcend personal advantage. But often the end of the enterprise which was the matrix of the relationship marks the beginning of the end of the relationship, and looking back one realizes that there was little personal involvement at all. This fact may be underlined by the difficulty, in meetings in later years, of sustaining more than superficial conversation—once the "remember when" routines have played out. The important thing to note is that *if* such friendships abide (and I have been the beneficiary of a number that have) it is because in the context of the common concern there was a flowering of personal concern. So basic to our fulfillment is a web of personal concern that we actually feel guilty when our relations have gone dead with those with whom in the past we spent much time or with whom we made common cause.

The true basis of personal concern is wrapped up in a Greek word for which we have no adequate English translation: *agápe*. That we cannot easily render it is probably just as well, because saying the word or even resolving to exercise it will not produce that which the word signifies. The Greek language, being somewhat more subtle than English, has three words for our one word "love." They are *eros, philia* and *agápe*. In the case of *eros* the object of the love is the source of the love; the loved one attracts love. In the case of *philia* an outside source nourishes the affection—a common interest or concern. In the case of *agápe* the source of the love is not apparent, but the occasion of it is the other's need of interest and concern.

All three have their place in the forming of a deep and abiding relationship, but of the three, *agápe* is the more basic because it in turn can produce or revive the other two. When I give my interest to another's concern two things are likely to happen, one to him and one to me: first, the warmth of my interest will cause his confidence and outgoingness to flourish, making him in fact more attractive personally and thus laying the foundation for *eros;* that is, I may come to like him for his own sake. Second, my selective attention to his interest will, in fact, develop an actual interest in what he's interested in, laying the foundation for *philia;* that is, his interest now becomes a common interest. *Eros* and *philia* are there or they are not; but *agápe* has creative power. It can bring into existence other bonds of affection which can then exist in their own right. But whence *agápe?*

It is strictly an "A.D." concept. There was no word for it, even in the Greek, before Christianity came into the world. St. Paul and St. John, who use it most in the New Testament, made use of an archaic word which was a synonym of *eros.* Paul's great redefinition and exposition of it is the classic passage in the First Epistle to the Corinthians: *

> Agápe is patient and kind,
>> is not jealous or boastful,
>> is not arrogant or rude.
>
> Agápe does not insist on its own way,
>> is not irritable or resentful,
>> does not rejoice at wrong, but
>>> rejoices in the right.
>
> Agápe bears all things,
>> believes all things,
>> hopes all things,
>> endures all things.
>
> Agápe never ends.

But where does it come from? On the surface, its source is not apparent, for by definition, it has no "angle." But to say that its source is not apparent is not to say that it has none. No love is ever unmotivated. "To win friends and influence people"? This can be a motive for outgoing focus on others, and can produce results. But then it is not *agápe* we are talking about, and in fact it is something a good deal less. If the reason we are attentive to others is to achieve or further a beneficial relationship or to "climb the social ladder," the quality of the thing is altered, and so sensitive are people to these things that sooner or later (and probably sooner) the motivation becomes apparent. This is not only true if we act on the coarse basis expressed by the man who said, "I always believe in being nice to people at least six months before I want to use them"; it can even be true when we are merely seeking to do our "daily good deed" or when we act as we do in order to reform the other. The self is still in it

---

* Here we avoid the "charity" of the King James Version because it is too narrow in connotation; and the "love" of the Revised Standard Version because it is too broad in connotation.

either in the form of advantage or of an enhanced sense of one's own goodness. In either case the impulse does not meet the test: "*Agápe* does not insist on its own way," or as in the King James Version, "seeketh not her own." Calculatedness is here ruled out; so is love from a pedestal (*"agápe* is not boastful" or "puffed up").

The *in order to* is the trouble. It is important to labor this because we have gotten into this subject in terms of a particular need of the self: in this case, loneliness. If the lonely person decides, or is helped to decide, that he ought to enter into others' concerns in order to be less lonely, a self-centered orientation has been encouraged and the quality of the outward concern has been marred. On the other hand—and there is a subtle but important difference—if the condition of loneliness can reveal the inadequacy of life without the sharing of the concerns for others, and thus a motive is sought which will result in the development of such concern as a habitual attitude, then what happens to his loneliness—and something will—entirely apart from particular results (and they will be ample) the person will have been changed and the highest form of love will be operating in his life.

Then what *is* the motive for *agápe*? Earlier we noted that as a concept for which there is a word it came into the world with Christianity. When people have a thing as a reality they are usually able to form a concept for it and find a word for it. But what we mean by *agápe* was not in fact part of the pagan ethic of either Greece or Rome and not in its fullness part of the Hebrew ethic. It came into the world with Christianity because in Christ a new kind of love broke into the world. In Christ, God acts out His *agápe* love for us. In our meditation on the Cross in Chapter IV we have seen that God accepts us not because we are acceptable but because we need acceptance. He loves us, not because we are lovable, but because we need love. And, as we have already seen, our response in gratitude to this kind of treatment by God is to pass on this accepting love to those around us. *The ultimate source of our* agápe *love is the love of God for us.* This is the ultimate source of it in contemporary men of good will who know not its source but who, in fact, have been deeply informed by it simply because they are part of a Christian culture. If this is the source even when we don't know it, how much more effective can it be in a given life when there is a conscious recognition of it.

If we meet others where they are because God meets us where we are, then we are relating ourselves to them on the deepest level, and in the most convincing and humble way. Then it is not *in order that* they may respond. We have already received our reward in what God does for us. Whatever good, in fact, results in the other or flows to us is in the class of those "other things" which shall be added. Gone will be the self-consciousness which so often accompanies our strained efforts to establish bridge-heads toward other people. Gone is the evidentness of our own need that can so inhibit the other's response. And much ameliorated will be the disappointments—and resulting cynicism—which often follow the failure of response in particular instances.

If good can come, and hawsers be thrown from life to life, by the right kind of concern in the heart of one of two parties involved, then obviously we can expect such relationships to abound in a community of people who know the love of God and are letting it flow out of their lives into the lives of their fellows. This is precisely what the Christian Church is meant to be. This is why Jesus was not content to establish an individual relationship with us, but laid the foundation of a fellowship. "I am the vine, ye are the branches," He said. And in a world hostile to them, the early Christians were marked off by this very thing: "See how they love one another!" was a contemporary appraisal. The author of an early Christian letter summed it up: "In this is love (*agápe*), not that we loved God but that he loved us and sent his Son to be the expiation for our sins. Beloved, if God so loved us, we also ought to love one another" (1 John 4:10-11).

That this writer felt it necessary to put this in exhortatory rather than purely descriptive terms shows that the Church has never in practice fully been what it is in principle. That should anticipate the skepticism of those whose experience of this or that church has not corresponded to Christ's aim for the Church. But our very disappointment with large reaches of the Church is due to the fact that we feel instinctively that the Church *ought* to be a community in which the deepest personal needs are met by love and acceptance. The only reason we have this norm by which to judge the Church in any particular place and time is that throughout the centuries the Church has sufficiently displayed this capacity that we are disturbed at failure of love in its members. And there is no doubt that throughout its history and in its manifold forms, the Church has kept this whole love relationship central in its message. It is the heart of the action of the sacraments, it is the key message of the pulpit. Unless we are to say that teaching has no relation to human understanding and action, we must confess that more love will come out of a particular life if it lives in this context, in which the message of love pouring into life is paramount, than if it is lived apart from this constant outpouring of message and reality. (This is a good part of the reason that a recent study could show 2¼ times less divorce among couples who worship together.) The failures of churchmen to love are in spite of this rich and constant stimulus to love.

We have seen that one of the things *agápe* does is to nourish common concern and that in turn common concern provides a matrix in which personal concern can develop. Not only does the Church preach and communicate *agápe*, it is also itself an enterprise which involves people in a common concern which is on a deeper and more abiding level than any other concern which can command the devotion of men.

This has been so from the beginning. In the third century St. Cyprian could write:

> This seems a cheerful world, Donatus, when I view it from this fair garden, under the shadow of these vines. But if I climbed some great mountain and looked out over the wide lands, you know very well what I would see. Brigands on the high roads, pirates on the seas, in the amphitheatres men murdered to please the applauding crowds, under all roofs misery and selfishness. It is really a bad world, Donatus, an incredibly bad world. Yet in the midst of it I have found a quiet and holy people. They have discovered a joy which is a thousand times better than any pleasure of this sinful life. They are despised and persecuted, but they care not. They have overcome the world. These people, Donatus, are the Christians—and I am one of them.

Christianity is not primarily a body of principles; it is primarily an enterprise, a movement. Any large movement can lift people out of themselves and their frustrations, increase their sense of power and personal significance and assuage their loneliness. We see this in any nation in time of war. And this is much of the appeal of Nazism and Communism to their adherents. We want no part of either; but we need something as vital and as corporate if we are to survive as a nation, if we are to lift individuals out of themselves. The atomization of our life has become so acute that in a city we do not even know our fellow apartment-dwellers—and, what is worse, we don't want to. The fact that so many evenings with the family or with friends are spent with the television set is not only a threat to that precious vehicle, personal conversation; it is also a compensation for the fact that the art of conversation is already largely lost—the bases of connection between people having largely disappeared.

This weakening of connections is traceable in good measure to the draining out of the common religious interest and conviction which used to be the spinal fluid of the body politic. More and more the religiousness has become implied rather than explicit and in large reaches of our family life it is not even implied. The matter of grace at meals is indicative. The long grace, accompanied by other prayers, before the family meal, gave way to a perfunctory exercise and this in turn has been eliminated by and large. Grace at meals is not in itself the most important thing in the world, yet its disappearance is a token of the disappearance of a whole level of meaning undergirding life and supporting it, one which provided the deepest common allegiance and outlook possible.

At the same time there are signs in our midst of the revival of Christianity as a movement. The draining off of the implied religiosity of the majority makes all the more evident the distinctiveness of the Christian minority. Thus Christianity is taking on more its original character as an active fellowship of people who put its cause ahead of all causes and see its spread as a common task. Wherever this is already happening there is evident a power which inspires and undergirds individual efforts and nourishes relationships between people. The converting and life-changing power of the group is a great deal more than the individuals themselves contribute: the total is greater than the sum of the parts. Christians believe that this *esprit de corps* is holy *esprit*, that is, *the Holy Spirit*.

The effectiveness of the Spirit in binding men together is shown by the fact that in the Christian cause men of the most diverse types and levels of society are united. Men and women whose interests diverge in every other way here find a tie that is firmer than the barriers which separate them.

This has been evident from the beginning. Among the early converts, says St. Paul, were "not many wise men after the flesh, not many mighty, not many noble" (1 Cor. 1:26-27). Soon, however, the new cause began to attract people of position, culture and education—though the people to whom they bound themselves (to the death, too, for that was always in the offing then) were not people with whom they otherwise would have been likely to mingle.

The Holy Spirit is the source of the *deepest* level of relationship because this concern is in the realm of the things that ultimately most matter. The Holy Spirit is the source of the *most abiding* level of relationship because this common cause lasts forever and, as we shall see in the next chapter, the relationship is not only with those we see and physically work and worship with, it is with the great "company of all faithful people" who have gone on before us in the Faith.

We found, a few pages back, that loneliness comes from the lack of deep and abiding basis of connection between people. The most profound Christian answer to loneliness, then, is the affirmation of the Creed "I believe in the Holy Ghost: the Holy Catholic Church; the Communion of Saints."

But, as has been suggested, this answer will not necessarily be *experienced* in every place which habitually recites those words. That this experience, so needful in our atomized culture, may more and more come to pass, something is required—both of those who would look to the Church for an answer to their personal loneliness and of those who make up our congregations.

To the first ("the outs") we must say: there *are* churches in which the working of the Holy Spirit is really evident and where one can really be grafted into living fellowship. Don't give up because you have run into a church which reminds you of the old taunt, "God's frozen people." Shop, if need be; but don't expect to be simply on the receiving line; come in an outgoing spirit—and be patient. Even the

Holy Spirit finds it hard to break through the walls people have around themselves. But when He does—that is, when they let Him—there is a ground of fellowship nothing else can equal. Countless folk have really experienced in the Church the fulfillment of Christ's expectation that His disciples would "receive a hundredfold now in this time houses and brothers and sisters and mothers and children. . . ."

To the second group ("the ins") we must say: ask these questions about your church: if a stranger came there, would he know that the Holy Spirit was at work by the warmth and genuineness of its fellowship? Would he find rea¹ belief in God easier because he experienced God's Spirit there? In short, is your church a place where loneliness is healed? There are such places; is yours one?

For people in both situations the right answer to these questions will be worked out in practice if they really "believe in the Holy Ghost," who in the phrases of a twelfth-century hymn, can

> Heal our wounds, our strength renew;
> On our dryness pour [His] dew . . .
> Bend the stubborn heart and will;
> Melt the frozen, warm the chill.

We have been talking about the sense of loneliness that points outward. There is the sense of loneliness that points inward. This is the less obvious, the more fragile of the two sentiments. But it is always there, though more often than not submerged in the unconscious. It is submerged for a number of reasons. Our very zeal for activity, our art of occupying all our waking moments with companionship or other distraction "keeps the lid on" such tender yearnings. In turn this zeal can be explained in large measure by an unconscious fear (or a conscious one, if we have faced the matter before) of recognizing the full implications of loneliness which even the closest of our fellow men cannot remove. There are those who would urge us to avoid this very dimension of experience. "Morbid introspection," they would call it. They would answer the question for us in advance: man has no meaning beyond himself as related to his fellows.

Yet down deep we know there is more. A good clue is the fact that all of us, especially those of us whose lives are tightly interlaced with those of others, really crave at times to be alone. Among the loveliest experiences one can contemplate are these: alone before the fireplace in one's study in the still watches of the night; alone in a roomette on a train, with three or four hours of uninterrupted travel ahead; alone in the sun by an inaccessible mountain lake; alone sitting in a quiet old church. Now the reality does not always live up to the expectation (because, left to one's own thoughts, one is sometimes visited by various demons of insecurity and so welcomes the end of the experience and eagerly embraces the distraction which activity or companionship brings). But the joy of aloneness has been often enough known that the validity of the experience can hardly be questioned. *We are meant to have some life with ourselves,* and there is a kind of loneliness—all the deeper because it is less patent—that besieges us if we are denied it.

But time spent alone can be a dangerous thing. If a man cultivates inwardness, he will make conscious to himself that which he unconsciously knows: that he is really united—to the core of his being—with no one. Then he will feel really alone. No one really knows him, and he really knows no one else. More than that, he will find that—much as he knows about himself—he does not really know *himself.* This may make himself more generous in his judgments of others and their motives, and less sure (positively and negatively) of his self-appraisals: he can say with St. Paul, "I do not even judge myself" (1 Cor. 4:3). But at the same time he may feel a sense of being hooked to nothing—that is, "unhinged." If he comes to this realization, he has introduced nothing new into his psyche—though the conscious thought may be new to him. This is a real crisis. It may mean the tottering of a house of cards. *Or*, it may mean the opening of the door to the deepest reality which can come into his life—*the practice of the presence of God.*

For God *does* know us. It is He "unto whom all hearts are open, all desires are known, and from whom no secrets are hid." He knows us and our true end is to know Him. He —in person—is the real answer to our most inward loneliness. It is the need for fellowship with Him that accounts for our so often undefined yearning which no human companionship can erase. This is what St. Augustine knew when he exclaimed, "Thou, O Lord, hast made us for Thyself, and our hearts are restless until they find their rest in Thee."

Such considerations are the deepest offense to the secular physicians of the soul. To them this is "escapism." It *is* mysticism and so great is their distaste for this aspect of the Christian religion that by a revealing metonomy they often label the whole of supernatural religion as "mysticism." There can be a wrong escapism in religion (more about this in the next chapter); but if God is the ultimate Reality and we are His creatures, then finding our grounding in Him is escape from the falsities of merely man-made prescriptions for our destiny. Christians believe that God is personal. The reasons for this belief are discussed more fully in Chapter X; but entirely apart from the logic of these reasons, we know that the personal encounter with God, the love of God, and mystical union with God, has been the experience of countless souls throughout the whole Judaeo-Christian tradition. To write this off as escapism or as a neurotic expression is to write off many (including Jesus, Who, in His humanity, showed forth a life in the most intimate union with the Father) whose "integration" and "right adjustment" is even more evident than that of those who label as illusory and morbid the search for a true vertical dimension in life.

Morbid indeed can be solitary meditation which ends with self. Wholesome indeed is solitary meditation the end of which is God. Wholesome in the literal sense: for only conjoined to God are we whole. Each of us has a God-shaped blank in his heart.

To sum up, the fullest answer to loneliness is threefold:

> The inter-personal experience of *agápe* love, an experience grounded in God's love for us shown forth in Christ;
>
> The corporate experience of fellowship in the Church, an experience grounded in God the Holy Spirit;
>
> The inward experience of God, an experience which God offers us as Father.

Father, Son and Holy Ghost: this for Christians is the fullness of God. We are meant to experience the fullness of God. Our loneliness is the God-given thirst that makes us ill-content with anything but Living Water.

# Chapter IX

## *DESPAIR*

A MAN CAN be loneliest at the moment of death, and the thought most calculated to make a man feel lonely is the thought of death. This explains a certain type of humor. We generally laugh at the mere mention of an undertaker or a coffin. Humor is a very common way of bridging an incongruity. Our risibilities support us as we skim over the surface of a deep issue. This also explains why at a wake or its modern equivalent it is easier to talk about anything else in the world than the actual matter at hand, namely, that someone is dead. And this is why it is the custom these days, more often than not, to conceal from a dying man the fact of his impending death, even to the extent of discouraging the call of a priest or a minister. If a man knows that he is going to die, the closest fellowship with his intimates cannot erase the fact that he will die alone.

But every man knows that his time will come—and knows it all the time. A man may be fairly successful in keeping such thoughts out of his conscious mind, but the pervasive nature of the realization in his unconscious levels is indicated by "outcroppings" from time to time—a mixture of thought and feeling which sometimes forces itself to the surface and makes him shudder as the significance of a tangible present reality is assailed by a vivid sense that all that he now enjoys is *contingent,* that these things and the like of them will pass away.

There are, of course, two ways to deal with such thoughts.

One is to sweep them away or avoid them by distraction. But, as in the case of a sense of guilt, this method does not get rid of the deep uneasiness. The other way is to face soberly and frankly the fact and significance of death, and the bearing that it has on all that we do now. This latter approach is very dangerous unless there are answers to the problem so faced. And it is the real suspicion—often even a real conviction—that there are no answers, which makes us adopt the first, rather than the second, remedy. For those for whom there are no answers, preoccupation with death is indeed morbid; it need not be morbid if our thinking and convictions go *beyond* death.

The difference which convictions about answers beyond death can make is pointed up by the fact that in the Judaeo-Christian tradition we have been taught to think about death frankly, to pray *Lord, let me know mine end* and *teach us to number our days*. One of the things for which people earnestly prayed in the ages of faith was to be delivered *from sudden death*. Today men would tend to pray for what amounts to the opposite—we even express gratitude that the deceased did not know his fate, that he passed on quickly. Formerly a man prayed to be delivered from sudden death so that he might know that he was dying and be given time to make as real as possible for himself the answers which lay beyond death. Modern man, aided by the art of the funeral director's words and deeds, glides over even the fact of death itself. Circumlocutions even avoid the word. Christian tradition faces death as fact. On this score, as on many others, it is more realistic than the secular culture which so prides itself on its realism.

*Now in the midst of life we are in death.* And if we can discern what it is that really underlies the fear of death, we will have identified an important aspect of our anxiety in life. One factor immediately suggests itself, in the light of

the ground we have already covered. The believer consciously—and even the unbeliever, unconsciously—senses the
truth of the dictum *after death, the judgment.* So the fear of
death is often another form of expressing a sense of guilt.
The feeling that one is "not right" is underlined in the context of death. Facing up to One Who is perfect righteousness,
with all one's masks removed, is a terrifying prospect. Ever
since Adam donned the fig leaf, men have been mask-makers.
Man knows that the profound colloquialism "you can't take
it with you" includes these masks. It has been assumed that
enlightened religion has no room for the wrath of God, yet
it is difficult to escape this motif as one pictures himself
facing God, pure goodness, just as he is: we can feel the reality of the medieval hymn *Dies irae*—

> Day of wrath! O day of mourning! . . .
> What shall I, frail man, be pleading? . . .
> When the just are mercy needing? . . .
> Lo! the book, exactly worded, wherein all hath
>     been recorded . . .
> When the Judge his seat atttaineth and each hid-
>     den deed arraigneth . . .

There is no one so sophisticated that these simple direct
phrases do not import some meaning to him.

If a man is convinced that there is no God, or no personal
God (One Who is at all concerned with what he does or
doesn't do), then he would seem to be freed from this fear;
but he really isn't, because even in his own terms he is confronted with the fear that the symphony of his life will be
ending on a sour note. He cannot but sense the inadequacy,
the shoddiness, the unworthiness that has characterized so
much of what was the only life that he had to live. This, too,
is the judgment. And if to relieve himself of even this stric-
ture, he has reconciled himself to the view that there is no
norm for his life which brings him under judgment, that
what he does does not really matter in either eternal or tem-

poral terms, then he has visited himself with an even deeper basis of anxiety—and this is one which is perhaps the most profound level underlying the fear of death—and one which plays its part in the depths of all of us: the sense of *meaninglessness*.

In short, a man's dilemma is this: if God is, and there is a life to come, the thought of death creates uneasiness because of the problem of guilt; if God is not, and there is no life to come, then the thought of death creates uneasiness because of the problem of meaninglessness. We have already discussed the Christian answer to the problem of guilt. We now turn to the problem presented by the other horn of the dilemma. It is not that the other discussion is for those who believe and this one for those who do not; because our convictions and inner attitudes are not as easily separated as this. Many an unbeliever is haunted by a sense of guilt, many a believer is haunted by a sense of meaninglessness—illogical as these two reactions, respectively, may be in the light of the professed credo of each type.

A full recognition and acceptance of the meaninglessness of life would have as its fruit the emotion of despair, but as has been suggested, men do not often face the full implications of their basic ideas. Many people their whole lives long have assumed the meaningfulness and ultimate importance of contingent things in the passing show and have never consciously raised the fundamental question, have never asked the big "So what?".

Suppose a baby were born on a giant airplane which kept circling the earth, never landing because it was supplied with gasoline and provisions from the air. As the child grew, he would develop a sense of security because of the reliable arrangement of the cabin: the family eats in one corner, his toys are in another, his little bed is in another corner, etc. But he eventually grows up enough to be able to look out the window. What a shock—everything is secure inside, but what is the whole thing attached to? The sense of the great abyss under life reflects a measure of maturity: people who still think the little meanings, the little securities, are adequate are still children no matter how old they may be in years. This is the moment of maturity, religiously speaking. It is both a moment of great opportunity and a moment of danger. For our airborne friend, his raising of this question is a moment of opportunity because at this point he would find relevant a consideration of the problems of aerodynamics and, with the proper tutelage, come in due time not only to an intellectual understanding of what it is that does support the airplane, but also appreciate the absolutely basic place of aerodynamics in his life on the plane. On the other hand, the child's realization of the apparently unsupported character of his life in the plane could result in a serious traumatic shock if he could not understand nor trust the principles on which his security rests.

So, too, in life. When once in a life the really big question is asked, two alternatives are opened up: a profound faith—or despair. The person who has never asked this question in one way or another does not have a really mature faith because, although he may profess belief in God and in the things of eternity, God is for him simply another being beside other beings, eternity is just more time after this present time has run out. But on the other side of this basic question, God is either the ultimate Ground of all being or nothing, Eternity is that which gives meaning to time now or else it is nothing. So here we are dealing with the ultimate religious question. That is why there is a sense in which the atheist in despair is more religious than the conventional churchman. He has raised and faced the ultimate religious question and thus is nearer to the true God (Who is ultimate or not at all) than the person who has never seen the critical nature of the ultimate question and for whom God is one of many aspects of life, simply one of the claimants for his interest and concern and allegiance. This can be seen by the fact that if and when the atheist comes to faith, he will come to the matter in a more basic way than the person who has apparently never doubted. For him it is an "all or nothing" matter. Just as Jesus saw the harlot as nearer the Kingdom of Heaven than the righteous ones (because there is a good chance that the person in a state of obvious sin will see the basic need of repentance), so, too, the person who has faced the question of ultimate meaning and has for the time being come out with a negative answer is nearer to God than the person who has never raised the ultimate question and in whose life God's place is part of a polytheism of allegiances.

We have been talking as though the ultimate issue between meaning and meaninglessness is that of God or no God. It is; yet, more precisely, the issue focuses on the matter of time and eternity, and in personal terms, on the question of eternal life. One cannot raise the question of eternal life basically as long as one thinks that the passing show is quite adequate and has its own self-authenticating meaning. As long as a woman can spend all of her spare time and waking hours (beyond the minimum of what it takes to keep daily life pulled together) working on committees of the local women's club (perhaps propelled by the expectation that she will in due time become president of the club) the question to which we are here addressing ourselves may not disturb her. But if something enters to arrest her enthusiasm and dampen her hopes and she pauses long enough in her momentum to ask "So what?", and having been confronted with the suspicion that perhaps none of it matters, she lets her thoughts turn to life generally and by a sort of relentless logic begins to suspect that *nothing* matters—then she is facing the religious question with which we are here concerned. If she does not know the answer to that question or perhaps concludes that "nothing does," then she knows what despair means. Such an answer is the maximum of anti-religiousness because the question she has asked is the maximum of religiousness. That is why it has been very difficult for people to decide whether such a passage as the following from Ecclesiastes is really religious, though it is in the Bible:

> Vanity of vanities, saith the Preacher, vanity of vanities; all is vanity.
>
> What profit hath a man of all his labor which he taketh under the sun?
>
> One generation passeth away, and another generation cometh: but the earth abideth for ever.
>
> The sun also ariseth, and the sun goeth down, and hasteth to his place where he arose.
>
> The wind goeth toward the south, and turneth about unto the north; it whirleth about continually, and the wind returneth again according to his circuits.
>
> All the rivers run into the sea; yet the sea is not full: unto the place from whence the rivers come, thither they return again.
>
> All things are full of labor; man cannot utter it: the eye is not satisfied with seeing, nor the ear filled with hearing.
>
> The thing that hath been, it is that which shall be; and that which is done is that which shall be done: and there is no new thing under the sun.
>
> Is there any thing whereof it may be said, See, this is new? it hath been already of old time, which was before us (1:2-10).

True, the author does not provide a very satisfactory answer for the problem he raises, but it is a religious work because it raises the religious issue which is every man's basic question. It is not merely the question of the man who wants things that he can't get (which can produce the frustration which we have already analyzed); it is also the question of the man who has gotten all that he can imagine is worth while, and then senses that none of it is worth while. "So I was great, and increased more than all that were before me in Jerusalem: . . . whatsoever mine eyes desired I kept not from them, I withheld not my heart from any joy . . . Then I looked on all the works that my hands had wrought, and on the labor that I had labored to do: and, behold, all was vanity and vexation of spirit, and there was no profit under the sun" (Eccles. 2:9-11).

As such, this is despair. And there is no further word beyond this, unless two things be true: first, that our own personal lives do not come to an end, that is, that we have eternal life; and second, that temporal events in this life have a place in the total meaning of things, that is, in eternity. We can see the importance of both of these elements if we note the effect on life now, when the world-view of a culture lacks either one of the elements. In a Marxist culture, the first is denied (and hence the second is irrelevant): a man dies like a dog, hence the state outlasts him and, quite properly (on these premises), can push him around. The individual does not matter. His little hopes and fears have no place in the scheme of things. In oriental cultures (before the time that Western influence had become marked) there was a belief in eternal life, but the second element was missing: the here-and-now had no real significance. The main object of life for those who were religiously serious was to pass beyond the specific and the temporal to the abstract and eternal; being absorbed into the over-soul was to achieve fulfillment. Thus in the India and the China of yore the temporal conditions of life here and now were unimportant. There was no zeal for progress to make things more livable for the mass of men because this life was unimportant and not worth the effort of redeeming. The significance of individual life, on the one hand, and the dynamic for progress, on the other—both of which have been characteristic of Western civilization—have their well-spring in a view of life in which the individual is ultimately significant, since he has an eternal destiny, and in which this world was seen as having a real meaning in connection with that destiny.

The Christian Faith supplies both of these conditions. It says that life now is meaningful, and every particular of it, because those that are doing the living are meaningful—and each one ultimately so—and because the day-to-day events in personal life and in social history have a significant part to play in the whole eternal drama. How this is so involves us in one of the most difficult aspects of Christian theology. But first let us turn to the prime requisite element of meaningfulness, namely, the fact of eternal life for the individual. Even before we do that, we should face a question which stands on the threshold in the minds of most moderns: isn't it more important to concentrate on life now, letting whatever lies ahead take care of itself? Are not thoughts of heaven an escape device to avoid facing reality?

It is not well to brush aside such questions or even attempt to answer them without recognizing the measure of truth which they express. Religion *can* serve as just such an escape device and can distract interest and energy from the task at hand. We can even concede the Marxists' charge that religion is an opiate of the people (provided we can render "is" as "can be"). Religion has offered "pie in the sky, bye and bye" as the compensation for privation now. But the real answer to the objection is that a sound religion need not do this. A religion which has heaven and earth in the right relationship is vitally concerned with life now and can provide a perspective on life now that gives it its fullest meaning and saves it from the meaninglessness that is the logical consequence of believing that this life is all there is. More than that, it can give a proper proportion to all the factors and values which compete in their claims of promise in the present life.

The value of a stock or bond does not depend only on its annual yield. An equally important factor is the number of

years it is likely to pay dividends. A share of oil stock yielding ten dollars per year from properties due to be drained
out in three years is worth at the most thirty dollars. A share
of telephone stock yielding ten dollars per year—since the
telephone, we fear, is here to stay—is worth a good deal
more. So you will weigh out things quite differently depend-
ing upon whether you think it's all over in a few short years
or whether you believe that you will abide as a person forever. The relative importance of things is altered by whether
life can be conceived of in the long view or in the short
view. For example, if men and God last forever and nations
come and go, each individual is really more important than
the state, and it is quite natural for people brought up on
such convictions to provide a Bill of Rights, just as it is quite
natural for a culture which has decided that the individual
is through when he is put in the ground to regard the
interests of a state as paramount over the evanescent individual. If kindness and sacrifice are eternally validated, then
it is much more logical to practice them to one's present
hurt than if the man who has lived for others and the man
who has lived for himself both have as their destiny extinc-
tion after a few short years. If personal relationships extend
into eternity and if in the life to come there is infinite opportunity for the further development of personal relations,
then even passing contacts with other human beings have a
value that they would not have if they can only be conceived
of as "ships passing in the night."

The argument that we should concentrate on the *now* and
not be distracted from our concern for the same by thoughts
of an after-life is based on the assumption that the present
life and the life to come (if it exists at all) are related in
a "straight line"—that eternity begins when this life is over.
As a matter of fact, we are in eternity now. Eternity represents another whole dimension which intersects our tem-

poral life, which judges it, which supports it, which gives it meaning. *To live in eternity is to live in depth now.* It is to live taking into account the full scope of reality rather than merely the flat view of the world which secularist thought assumes. The word secularism itself is revealing here. It derives from *sæculum*, "age." Secularism is "this-age-ism," "this-is-all-there-is-ism," "there-isn't-any-more-ism." The same root is used in a phrase which aptly characterizes the way of looking at things in full dimension: the phrase which ends the many traditional Christian prayers, *per omnia sæcula sæculorum,* variously translated "world without end," "forever and ever," "throughout all ages of ages." This does not simply mean *a long time*—it means a different kind of *now*. Consciously living in eternity in the midst of time makes a difference in two ways: first, as we have seen, a different norm of judgment and evaluation enters the picture if we see all things *sub specie æternitatis,* in the light of eternity; and, second, we enter a larger realm of reality, strengthened and nourished by the sense of the presence of God, the communion of saints, and all the spiritual forces which are loyal to God. In the most discouraging situation we are enabled to feel the force of Elisha's word to his servant (when the Lord had opened the eyes of the young man): "Fear not, they that be with us are more than they that be with them."

There are secularists who recognize that some "purchase" is needed on this present life, some scope of meaning beyond the threescore and ten, and propose two solutions other than life eternal. Until recently, when it was generally assumed that "inevitable progress" was an unchallengeable axiom, it was frequently said that meaning was given to human life by the fact that in each generation we could contribute to the progress of mankind and thus each have our part in the perfect consummation which lay ahead up the road for some future generations. Granted this particular view of history (which the facts render dubious), one is reminded of the story of the great castle which a ruthless prince had erected at the top of a lofty mountain, the road to which was built out of the bones of the hundreds of men who lost their lives in its construction. If we deny those who give their lives along the road any measure of personal participation in the fulfillment it is difficult to see how any personal meaning has been imported into their lives, especially since we have no way of knowing what kind of people will inherit the fruits of their labors. In any case, if the latter themselves have no personal future or transcendent meaning, their supposed future happy estate, a few short years for each generation, cannot be the basis of importing meaning backwards into the lives of their predecessors in the race.

The same is true of the argument that we receive sufficient meaning for our lives because we live in the memory of others and in the influence which we leave behind us. One of my first "shocks," comparable to that of the child who grew old enough to look out of the airplane window and observe the abyss beneath, came when a college friend whom I was visiting for the week end told me about his father, a prominent trial lawyer, who had died several years before. He gave me for my inspection a scrapbook which contained numerous clippings reporting his court appearances, motions, briefs, and public statements. I thumbed through the news stories, the frequent banner headlines, and the pictures of the counselor in action in court, with considerable interest, very much impressed by his achievements. Then it suddenly dawned on me that I had never even so much as heard of the man before. I further reflected that probably very few people so much as thought about him anymore. The transience of things in this life and of the memory of lives lived, struck me with great force. True, this man had had some bearing on the lives of others, including, doubtless, that of his son. But if those in whose lives he could be presumed to have had some influence also have no destiny beyond the grave, then even the influence that he exercised becomes ultimately meaningless. Regardless of the network of lives and of mutual influence, if no one life has a lasting destiny, then zero plus zero still equals zero (and it doesn't matter how many ciphers one adds to the left side of the equation, the answer is still the same).

More logical than these "half-way houses" in the attempt to construct meaning is the straight "existentialism" which frankly denies that there are any larger meanings, denies that there is anything but a succession of particular moments, particular configurations of inward emotion or outward relationship. Jean-Paul Sartre draws the conclusion ruthlessly: if there is no God, then there is no ethic or right or wrong, there is no meaning. And this is *despair*. Any who are familiar with the drama or art which is the expression of existentialist or other positivist world-views can see meaninglessness writ large—despair in its stark reality.

The only genuine alternative to despair is the Christian Faith that personal life is ultimately significant, both in its abiding structure and in its every individual moment—because the individual lives on as a person forever, and because there is continuity in every relationship between men and between men and God. Of no personal relationship can it be said "there is no future in it." Every action has abiding consequences right into eternity and every human contact is part of a web of relationships that will be continually in the process of development, enrichment and redemption through all the years ahead, during life and beyond the grave. The degree to which one individual comes to know another is that much ground gained in the completion of the whole of God's plan, in which ultimately we shall all know ourselves and each other as we are all now known by God. No measure of order made out of chaos is ever lost ground in terms of the total project which is the will of God for men. Every expression of love builds up the Kingdom of God and strengthens, to a small degree at least, the bonds between human personalities, which are meant to be fully and richly related forever.

This view of things rests upon an understanding of immortality which is unique to the Biblical faith. Characteristically, all men everywhere have had an abiding yearning for fulfillment beyond themselves, and the universal character of this yearning is one reason why it is more plausible to assume the continuity of life beyond the grave than to assume the opposite. For every universal human yearning has a matching fulfillment: men are hungry—there is such a thing as food (whether or not every man at all times can have his fill); men yearn for sexual fulfillment—there is such a thing as sex (though again not every individual at every point in his life has satisfactory sex relations); so if there is a general yearning for fulfillment beyond the grave—it is not implausible to assume that there is some corresponding reality which has evoked this yearning. But the view of the nature of this fulfillment is quite different in non-Christian religions and we should develop this contrast somewhat because many Christians tend to assume a view of the life to come which is in fact more in line with non-Christian conceptions than with Biblical ones, and because the full answer to the personal problem we are now considering—despair and meaninglessness—depends upon the full-bodied, authentic Christian view.

We have seen, in considering the problem of inhibition, the dangers that arise from the soul-body distinction, especially when the implication is drawn that the soul is good and the body is bad. Oriental religions generally press this point to the limit and say that salvation consists of getting out of the body completely and being all soul. In this life the more that one can escape from particular existence into a generic existence, the more one's thoughts can pass from the specific to the abstract, the more the personality can pass from the conscious to the unconscious, the nearer one is to ultimate fulfillment. The ultimate outcome for the blessed is a state of absorption into general spirit (sometimes called "over-soul"), a state in which all individuality is lost and in which consciousness disappears. In other words, the proper direction of life is for persons to become less and less personal, less and less individual.

The Christian idea is as opposite as it can be. The direction of life is for persons to become more and more themselves, to express their own individual and peculiar gifts more and more adequately and fully. Under this conception, in the life to come there is a continuity of individual human personality and indeed its very peculiarity and individuality is conceived of as being heightened rather than diminished. As we have suggested above, the two quite different ways of viewing human destiny bear directly on two quite different ways of evaluating individual personality here and now. (This is a good illustration of the fact that it does make a difference what one believes—and what whole cultures believe.)

Now the continuity and further development of human personality requires a means of expression and communication, a means of individuation. We may admire the spirit of another person, but, in fact, we know nothing directly of his spirit. We hear physical noises uttered by his physical vocal chords, we see physical facial expressions and physical gestures. We are in touch with his spirit through his body. Indeed, we don't know anything about a soul apart from the body; all we know is a total psychosomatic personality with which we are in touch. The Christian Faith teaches that in the life to come, too, there is a suitable means of expression, communication, and individuation. The life to come, just as life at its best now, is not general and abstract, it is individual and social. In our earnestness in affirming this, we use a phrase which admittedly has caused a good deal of difficulty for people, but which, when explained, can be seen as a most suitable expression of this vital feature of eternal life. The phrase is *the resurrection of the body*. Obviously, this does not mean that the particular body that I now have will continue into eternity—its elements hardly last seven years in fact. But it does mean that there will be a continuity of my personality and that a means of expression and relationship at least as suitable as my body is now for present purposes, will be provided into all eternity by a God Who values human personality and individuality even higher than we do at our best.

Yet the American folk theology about death and the life to come is of quite a different order. Assuming that in their advertising funeral directors, cemeteries, mausolea, and headstone manufacturers want to stress those things that the public would like to hear, we must infer that in the "rest" and "peace" which is expected and equated to dignified oblivion, any life which the soul might be conceived of as having is indeed vague, disembodied, and abstract. And this is to be the fate of the righteous and unrighteous alike, apparently. However suitable such notions may be to the premises of oriental religions, they are entirely out of line with the Christian hope of the life to come or the Christian evaluation of the life that now is.

True, the Christian Faith is not equipped with a blueprint of the world to come, nor are we able to portray it with even the degree of clarity now achieved on a television screen. But certain things connected with the life to come are fundamental to the whole Christian view of life. First, each individual, with his own peculiar make-up, is precious to God and it is the will of God that that individual remain himself and become more and more himself. Second, one of the ends of creation—perhaps the chief end—is the achievement of fellowship between each individual and God and between each individual and every other individual with whom he is in contact. Third, the norm of the ideal that God would see fulfilled in personal relations is *agápe* love. Fourth, whether an individual will so behave that he is developing his relationship with God and creating order out of the chaos of human relationships is always a matter of the individual's free choice; God will not force anyone to want Him or to serve anyone else. Fifth, the freedom which God has given us implies our freedom to make selfish choices, indeed most hateful and destructive ones.

Now these premises set the stage for the Christian understanding of the life to come. Heaven is the state of being in the right relation to God and to other personalities. Hell is being shut off from God and the defiance of His will for our personal relations. Hell is a necessary implicate of our freedom. God so respects our freedom that He will not force us even into heaven. We are so free that we can shake our fists at Him throughout all eternity if we wish. He does not so much put us in hell as we put ourselves there. The door to hell is locked from the inside. He seeks us, He knocks on the door. He utilizes His tremendous spiritual resources, including the spirits of those who are on His side, to attract us out of the box in which we have locked ourselves. At the time of death very few of us will have fully turned to God, that is, will have fully let His light into all the dark corners of our personalities, will have fully yielded up to Him our will. There are "pockets of resistance" in most of us, areas that we regard as our "own business." If we basically have other gods than Him, then it is quite possible that we will not have the will to go at the cleansing of our lives, the will to put Him in charge of them. Or, to change the figure, we may have erected such fortifications around ourselves by our rationalizations and defenses that we will hardly hear

His knocking and that of those He has enlisted in the effort to bring us around. How long we can safely put off our reform, how long we can delay our turning to God, and still hope to hear His call and have the strength to turn, is a question which can only be answered after the event. Above Niagara Falls a few miles there is a sign which reads "No Boating Beyond This Point." A strictly accurate mind might protest that it is really impossible to define that point as the one beyond which boating is unsafe. After all, it would depend upon the flow of the current that particular day, upon the size of the boat, upon the strength of the rowers. Yet there *is* a point. And there may be such a point in the life of each of us. To pass this point is to be lost. (But, of course, even here we could set no limits to God's grace, exercised with ingenuity and perseverance and imaginativeness. Maybe somewhere deep in eternity the time will come when He will have found a way of attracting all to hear Him and to turn to Him, and when there will no longer be any "pockets of resistance" against Him and He will be "all in all.")

On the other hand, if He is essentially our first allegiance, we will be sufficiently in touch with His own direct confrontation (seeing then face to face as we now see through a glass darkly) that we will keep at the work of completing our redemption, of giving up one by one our little idolatries, of opening up to His searching and healing Light all the dark closets of our lives. It is this experience which St. Paul describes in these words:

> For no other foundation can anyone lay than that which is laid, which is Jesus Christ. Now if any one builds on the foundation with gold, silver, precious stones, wood, hay, stubble—each man's work will become manifest; for the Day will disclose it, because it will be revealed with fire, and the fire will test what sort of work each one has done. If the work which any man has built on

the foundation survives, he will receive a reward.
If any man's work is burned up, he will suffer
loss, though he himself will be saved, but only as
through fire (1 Cor. 3:11-15).

This means that there will be plenty to do in the life to
come, plenty to give individual personalities scope for the
exercise of their unique personal gifts. As to one's self, there
is the task of completing one's salvation, the opportunity of
deepening in the knowledge of God, grasping more and
more of the awe and wonder of Him and of all His works,
which will be increasingly understood as the barriers to one's
sight and response are removed one by one. As to others,
there is the task of sharing in their redemption, seeking to
remove barriers to understanding and fellowship which are
part of the situation with which we began in the new en-
vironment, seeking to help others with their own problems
without violating their freedom, helping loose the hold of
the idols, all the while entering more and more into the secret of the other, seen in the light of God. Then there will
be the opportunity of knowing the beauty of the glorified
personalities of the saints, the great ones of all ages—a knowledge which will be in itself a judgment upon us and our
own unredeemed aspects, at the same time an encouragement
and an attraction to the beauty of holiness. And then our
concerns for those still in the earthly race will by no means
be dimmed, but will be increased as we know more and
discern better, and see the issues of human life more clearly.
This is the communion of saints in action. It is the fullness
of meaning. It is "what the whole show is about." It is for
this that God created the world.

What does this have to do with the meaning of our lives
now? Here we must go back and stress the concurrence of
the life to come and the life that is, the concurrence of eternity and time. All of this that we have been describing in

terms of the life to come is in fact a description of the meaning of life now. Though God is now "invisible, . . . light inaccessible, hid from our eyes," though now we see through a glass darkly, the meaning of our existence on this earth is precisely the same: it is the task—and opportunity—of knowing God and accepting Him more and more as the center of our allegiance, and of serving Him, through the use of our own particular gifts, more and more in loving personal relationships. Our situation is basically the same as in the life to come. Even if we have decided to put God first (that is, have been converted) there still is a great deal more work to be done in realizing in every aspect of our personalities the full implications of this decision; and there are endless opportunities for building deeper and richer relationships around us. With us, as a present reality, are the same resources: the grace of God, the example and the real fellowship of all those who have gone on beyond and those who are still in this earthly clime, whose Lord is the same, whose goal is the same.

It is in this spirit that the author of the Epistle to the Hebrews wrote: "Wherefore, seeing we also are compassed about with so great a cloud of witnesses, let us lay aside every weight, and the sin which doth so easily beset us, and let us run with patience the race that is set before us, looking unto Jesus the author and finisher of our faith" (12:1-2). We need not wait for the life to come to enter into the fullness of the meaning of eternal life. We can respond to the grace of God now to cleanse ourselves of idolatries, of anxieties, fears, faithlessness, and disloyalty. We can go to work now in numerous personal relationships to be a means of grace to others. We can share now the fellowship of the saints, entering more and more into a knowledge of their lives, confident that we are not exploring the experiences of past dead heroes but of the living, who, though unseen, are a heavenly "rooting section" as we "run the race that is set before us." Even

now, through individual effort or corporate action, we can
help provide the conditions which enable men to receive
grace. We can do this in every kind of endeavor, from ex-
tending the mission of the Church—to slum clearance, from
reconciling members of a family—to supporting the United
Nations: whatever will make more avaliable the means of
grace in human life anywhere. And since the life of each
individual person is forever, every single gain in this regard
has a permanent significance, an abiding consequence. The
redemption of each individual life and of our corporate relationships is a task that occupies both this life and the life
to come, on into eternity. All that is accomplished now is
accomplished, and its accomplishment now is of as much
significance as its accomplishment beyond the grave. This
view of things is what gives an ultimate meaning, grounded
in the deepest reality, to every moment of personal existence.

The urgency of the moment is lost upon us as we see the
years stretch out ahead of us. Thus, the contemplation of
death and judgment—and the life beyond—is a most practical
and realistic exercise for making our present activity as
worthwhile and meaningful as possible. If we are concerned
lest, "when the master of the house cometh . . . he find
[us] sleeping," if we are ready at any moment for judgment,
we will be as the wise virgins, with lamps alight and with
a good reserve of oil. Truly, now is the time of salvation, for
though the judgment is to come, the judgment is also now;
at every moment in God's eyes we are judged and are seen
as we are. It is as a guide for our *present* life that we can
profit from the words of an old prayer about death which
Jeremy Taylor wrote for the Visitation of the Sick, which in
its modern form reads:

> O God, whose days are without end, and whose
> mercies cannot be numbered; Make us, we be-
> seech thee, deeply sensible of the shortness and
> uncertainty of human life; and let thy Holy Spirit

lead us in holiness and righteousness, all our days:
that, when we shall have served thee in our generation, we may be gathered unto our fathers, having the testimony of a good conscience; in the
communion of the Catholic Church; in the confidence of a certain faith; in the comfort of a reasonable, religious, and holy hope; in favour with
thee our God, and in perfect charity with the
world. All which we ask through Jesus Christ our
Lord.

The answer to the problem of despair and meaninglessness
is "I believe in . . . the Resurrection of the body: And the
Life everlasting."

A few words about the concern with which we began: the
fear of death. We spoke of the reticence of so many people
today to allow a dying person to know that he really is
dying. There are exceptions. There are people whose relatives sense that they *can* face the fact of death and that this
reality need not be hidden from them. These are the ones
who, those close to them (even those who themselves have
not taken too seriously the dimension of eternal life) know
already, have a strength beyond death. The great difference
in the way that people die is a sign of the difference in the
way in which people live. The man who in his lifetime is
already living in eternal life knows Him in Whom he trusts,
who knows his vocation in terms of the eternal meanings of
God's purposes in the interrelationship of men in and
through Him, who lives daily under judgment and accepts
himself daily through God's accepting grace—such a man
has died already to those things that would keep one in hell,
or cabin one in with the things which die. If one lives for
things which die, one dies with them. If one lives for those
things which are eternal, one already has eternal life. One
who has died already to the things which die, need never

die again, need never fear death. Too occupied with the
tasks to which God has set them here to yearn for death,
they yet look forward expectantly and triumphantly to the
fuller life that is beyond. They know that when they are
freed from the limitations of earthly existence, they can even
more fully set themselves to the tasks which will not be new
tasks but will be fuller opportunities for the discharge of
those tasks that have been here grasped and here loved, tasks
which here have brought their reward in the deeper knowledge of God and the enriching of human relationships.

Those who call this kind of concern for eternity "escapism"
simply have not troubled themselves to understand it. We
can define religious escapism as escape from reality into illu-
sion. If reality is not whole without God and His part in
personal life, if the meaning of this life can only be seen in
the light of eternal life which interpenetrates this world, as
well as being a continuation of it, then entering into eternal
life now is an escape indeed. It is an escape from earthbound-
edness, from the futility, the cynicism and the despair which
are bound to come from a candid meditation on a conception of human life which ends with the grave, with no over-
arching meaning, with no permanence—in personal terms—
for the gains that are made in spiritual depth or interpersonal
width. The ignoring of eternal life is escapism indeed; it is
an escape *from* truth, an escape *from* the claims of the
Ground of our existence, an ostrich-like reaction to the real
meaning of the universe.

# Chapter X

## SPIRITUAL OASES

By this time we can see that the answers to each of our greater inner problems have one thing in common: they depend on taking into account a realm beyond sense and beyond human calculation. As we have just seen, this does not mean waiting for life hereafter; it means living *now* in a dimension in which the supernatural is known as interpenetrating the natural, operating within it and through it. The word from the book of Revelation, "Behold, I make all things new," can sum up what it is for each of the problems that makes the difference. The difference between fear and trust, between inhibition and true joy, between a sense of guilt and self-acceptance, between a sense of frustration and a sense of vocation, between loneliness and abiding fellowship, between meaninglessness and meaning—is the presence of the living God in His world.

Of course, God is present in any event. He is with the fearful no less than the secure. The difference between them is that the latter *knows* that God is, and has adjusted his priority scale accordingly. He is with the guilt-ridden no less than with the man who rightly accepts himself. The difference between them is that He is with the former as judge (though he know not Who judges him) while the latter lives in the confidence that He "taketh away the sins of the world."

Millions of people wrestle with their inner problems without taking into account the fact of God. If God is, this means that such people are trying to put together a jig-saw puzzle with a good portion of the pieces missing from the set.

There are many others, including some who have read this far, who know, intellectually speaking, what the Christian Faith is, and who may even know the relevance of that faith to various aspects of personal life, yet for whom God is not *real* enough to make any significant difference to their personal states. It is to them that this Chapter is directed. How can a man really *live* in the full dimension of a natural-supernatural world, right in the here-and-now?

It will help some be patient with themselves in this matter if we first see why it is so difficult today for an individual to perceive the reality of God.

No one lives in a vacuum. In general our value-patterns and the range of our interests, tastes, and perceptions are determined by our society or the subdivision of it in which we characteristically move. This is what by and large determines what is *real* for us. Picture a large mural covering the whole side of a wall. The lighting can be so arranged that certain figures in it are brought out vividly, others shade into insignificance and still others are blacked out. Now the fact is that for half a century the "lighting" in our culture has been such that things which make for material progress stand out vividly, things of earth which minister to the higher reaches of the human spirit are somewhat in the penumbra, and supernatural verities have been so dim that for many they are invisible.

God does not drop out of His world simply because men do not sense His presence nor see Him as behind and under the visible tokens of His creative power. In fact His material gifts are equally available to those who know who the Giver is and those who do not. "The rain rains on the just and the unjust." But the just are those who know whence the rain comes. The difference is in us not in Him. People who see no more than the "natural" live in a smaller world than those who sense the supernatural as well. In the words of Francis Thompson:

> The angels keep their ancient places;—
> Turn but a stone, and start a wing!
> 'Tis ye, 'tis your estrangèd faces,
> That miss the many-splendoured thing.

Now this sensing of the Divine, or what Brother Lawrence called "The Practice of the Presence of God," is an easier business when the explicit tokens of religion loom large in the whole cultural milieu. In medieval Chartres there was no doubt about what was the principal building in town. It was the cathedral, just as in colonial New England the meeting-house was beyond all doubt the principal place in any village. Today there are very few people in, say, Detroit who could tell you how to get to a cathedral.

So, too, with the realm of polite conversation. We may laugh at medieval speculations about how many angels can dance on the head of a pin, but in any event they were talking about angels, which are—at the least—the symbols of God's "on-the-job" action everywhere in the world. Arguments over a cracker-barrel in the general store about the precise mode of predestination may seem futile to us, but all the contenders were as one in assuming a God who had the reins in His hands. Today you may move in polite circles for a week and never hear God so much as mentioned—except as part of an expletive.

The renovation, the "respiritualizing," of our culture is, of course, an important task which should concern us all, but meanwhile we naturally ask, "if the salt lose its savor, where-with will it be salted?" The answer to this long-range question, as well as to our personal needs in such an age is this: we must find our place in a culture within a culture. We must resort to spiritual oases—to drink deeply of that which will enable us to survive in the spiritually arid desert of a secularized society. *They that wait upon the Lord shall renew their strength.*

This is one of the rôles of public worship—to provide a special atmosphere in which it is more possible to sense the reality of the living God. When someone says, "Oh, I can worship God anywhere," the answer is, of course, yes. But the next question to ask is "Do you?" It is much easier to feel God's presence and the reality of religious verities in a setting which intensifies our fragile perceptions, increases our spiritual sensitivities. When a magnifying glass is placed above a piece of paper in the sun, the amount of sunlight is not increased, but the effectiveness of the sun is—enough perhaps to burn a hole in the paper. So in worship "My soul doth magnify the Lord" (Luke 1:46), and "I will magnify thee, O God, my King" (Ps. 145). In worship we quite literally *magnify*, "make great," God in our lives.

At the least, regular habits of worship guarantee that we will be reminded of God from time to time, will hear information about Him and our relationships with Him. But a great deal more than this is involved. As we have seen in the case of each of the great problems of security, a good deal of the trouble is in the unconscious mind. It is there the most devastating fear resides, it is there that suppressed guilt feelings do their damage, and so on. Worship can deal directly with the unconscious.

Suppose one's physician discovered a serious internal infection. "I can operate," he says, "but it is a dangerous operation, due both to the location of the infection, and the danger of reinfection and of possible side complications." And just as the patient is quaking in his boots, the doctor adds, "But there is a ray that is often effective and that we can apply from the outside without opening you up. We can try that first, if you're willing to come every week for the treatments." There is little doubt that the patient would keep his weekly appointments.

Now if the unconscious is sufficiently infected, an "operation" may be necessary—this operation is called a psychoanalysis. But it is dangerous: there is a danger of reinfection as all the old material is pulled up into conscious mind; there are possible side complications, such as the development of new false attachments (for example, to the analyst) or the increase in self-concern, itself the root of most psychic imbalance. So if there is a way that we can fight the demons within without opening up the unconscious, a way that we can inject antibodies to "take on" the disturbing forces within, we should certainly resort to such a way ahead of what is the last resort, analysis.

Now worship is just such a way. Through it the symbols of security are sent through well-worn channels into the unconscious. Worship furnishes the unconscious with positive, life-giving forces to combat and "neutralize" the negative, death-dealing forces, which, left alone, accumulate and multiply there. Worship is, at the least, *mass-production psychotherapy*.

Let us examine a little more closely how this is so.

First of all, the church building itself provides surroundings which are "out of this world." We generally build our churches to look like nothing else. Whether cathedral or rural chapel, the church, both because it is "different" and because of hallowed associations, provides intimations of God's presence, assures us of the reality of the supernatural dimension in life by means which are deeply suggestive—to the unconscious even more than the conscious. The church spire itself symbolically (though not geographically) points to Heaven. For most of us it is usually much more difficult to sense the divine presence and to free ourselves from the "earth-bound" associations (for example, the individual personalities involved) in "informal worship" in a lounge, meeting room, or living room. On entering church we often feel as though we are brought into a searching yet sustaining Presence—and feel unclean—and cleansed.

Second, in church we grow quiet, as we rarely do these days. *The Lord is in His holy temple: let all the earth keep silence before him.* Outside, the pressures of activity—or reminders of activity—bar communication with our spirits. Holy quiet relaxes the barrier between conscious and unconscious. Expressive of this aspect of worship is the late Dr. Suter's beautiful prayer:

> O God of peace, Who hast taught us that in returning and rest we shall be saved, in quietness and confidence shall be our strength; By the might of thy Spirit lift us, we pray thee, to thy presence, where we may be still and know that thou art God. . . .

Third, the *action* in the service points beyond itself to the unseen mystery, stirring our spiritual imagination, the familiar tokens communicating directly to our inner selves. Whatever actions are familiar in the worshiper's tradition have power to communicate deeply, because "the grooves are cut." (This is why it is important to introduce children to the experience of the regular worship forms, instead of confining them to "children's services" specially designed for them.) Processions, the cross, the lighting of candles, signs of reverence to the altar, cross or Bible, kneeling or bowing for prayer, rising for praise, familiar hymns, chants and prayers, the presentation of alms (which are the tokens of our lives), and, of course, supremely, the holy things used in the central sacraments and mysteries of our Faith, the water, bread and wine—all these are carriers of meaning to the inner life.

The effectiveness of such channels may be illustrated by a common experience in the ministry to the sick. A semi-comitose patient who may not respond to conversation or informal prayer will often "come to life" when shown a cross, or the chalice and host, or when read prayers of great familiarity. These strike to the depths of his being and the assurance they bring reaches the whole self though the conscious mind be but little operative. Similarly, it is why during the last war so many chaplains from non-liturgical churches turned to sacramental forms in their ministry to men who were under intense strain and thus not particularly rationally receptive to "ideas." The dozens of altars set up along the beach-head by the chaplains at Dunkerque for Communion night and day spoke more basically to the situation than could have a dozen pulpits filled with silver-tongued preachers.

Now we are all sick in a measure, we are all under strain, and these same things can furnish our inner lives with healing, strengthening power. Considering the infection within, the new sources of infection all around us, who should ever miss a "treatment"?

But does not the very familiarity of these things breed inattention and lead to "routine" in worship? Yes—it can, but it need not do so; and here it should be said that in fact a certain amount of inattention contributes to the deep communicability of the familiar. It is part of our acute "mentalism" bred by the last two centuries of rationalism that makes us feel guilty if we are not following with our conscious minds the words and ideas of, say, the Psalms. Actually, half-attention, half-inattention enhances the communicability to the depths of the key-symbols in familiar material. A good example is the *Venite* ("O come, let us sing unto the Lord") sung in the public worship in a number of traditions. The very monotony of the chant helps soften the layer between conscious and unconscious. We saw how "therapeutic" are its key-ideas, how wholesome they are for our depths, when we considered the problem of fear: *Let us heartily rejoice in the strength of our salvation*—God is utterly reliable. *He is a great King above all Gods*—no other

forces can really hurt us, and devotion to Him can bring
into line all subordinate drives and interests. *In His hands
are all the corners of the earth*—He covers the whole of
reality, there is no place where we can go where He
isn't, no aspect of life to which He is not relevant. The world
has a shape, life has a meaning, there is something to count
on; *for He cometh, for He cometh to judge the earth.* But
He isn't just abstract principle; *we are the people of His
pasture, the sheep of His hand*—He is personally concerned
about every last one of us.

What healthier rays could be played into our depths?

But all of this may disturb the pious. "Do you mean to
say," they may ask, "that worship is just psychology? The
Church was at worship centuries before all this 'depth' business was so much as thought of." True, the churches have
been wiser than they knew in their use of externals and in
the ordering of the services. One is reminded of M. Jourdain
of *Le Bourgeois Gentilhomme* who one day looked up the
word "prose" in the dictionary and found to his surprise that
he had been speaking prose all his life. Regardless of the
concepts of nomenclature we associate with depth psychology, the Church over the centuries has had a very wide
clinical experience in the cure of souls, both through individual counseling and corporate action; and the response of
the worshipers has in itself been a significant formative influence in the development of liturgy and of the forms of
personal ministration.

Thus it should not surprise us that much in the traditional
modes of worship is good psychology. But, of course, it is
not *just* psychology. And this for two reasons: first, forms
of words and actions do not operate very well, even psychologically, apart from their communication of meaning; and
hence the important place that preaching and instruction
have in the life of the Church. The reason why the *Venite,*

for example, can communicate to the unconscious the ground of our security, is that concepts such as these have been explained tellingly—in sermons, in classes, in personal counseling. And if the words are to retain their fresh impact, they must be explicated again and again, in terms of the related and supporting concepts of theology and in terms of the manifold applications which personal and social problems suggest. This is in accord with St. Paul's statement of the rule of Christian worship: "I will pray with the spirit, and I will pray with the understanding also: I will sing with the spirit, and I will sing with the understanding also" (1 Cor. 14:15). In periods and in places where the ministry of the Word has been at a low ebb the liturgy has been a much less effective instrument for the healing and stabilizing of men. Yet it must be said that there have been periods in which it has been the only bulwark of a sound and realistic Christianity: for example, while in a good many places till recently the sufficiency of man to work out his salvation—and pretty much on a natural plane—was being proclaimed from the pulpit, yet in the service these sentiments were fortunately being contradicted by such phrases as "O Lord God, who seest that we put not our trust in anything we do," "O God . . . without whom nothing is strong, nothing is holy," ". . . forasmuch as without thee we are not able to please thee," and that phrase, so offensive during the optimistic decades that a large denomination excised it from its service book and college chapels generally dropped it: "There is no health in us."

Second, much more than the psychology is involved because God really acts from His direction as we approach Him in worship. Brought into our unconscious levels are not only these symbols of security, of acceptance and of fellowship (themselves important), but also the realities for which these symbols stand. God Himself as Father (source of our security), Son (source of our acceptance), and Holy Spirit (source of our fellowship)—God Himself actually visits us. God's outgoingness to usward is called *grace*. Our confidence that He so acts is expressed in the familiar canticle of worship (the passage from St. Luke's Gospel called "the Song of Zacharias") in which we sing:

> Blessed be the Lord God of Israel; for he hath visited and redeemed his people, . . .
> That we should be saved from our enemies, and from the hand of all that hate us;
> To perform the mercy promised to our forefathers, . . .
> To give knowledge of salvation unto his people for the remission of their sins,
> Through the tender mercy of our God; whereby the dayspring from on high hath visited us,
> To give light to them that sit in darkness and in the shadow of death, and to guide our feet into the way of peace (Luke 1:68-79).

The reality of this aspect of worship is hard for us to grasp because for a long time we have thought of worship only as *edification,* as something which inspires us, puts the right thoughts in our heads. And this attitude is part of a whole conception of God as a passive force or as a body of principles, leaving us to do all the acting in the work of our salvation. Such a conception of God is a truncated one, falling far short of the God of Biblical faith. People are quite right in fearing anthropomorphism and in hesitating to regard God as *a person* Who is simply bigger and more powerful than other persons and Who operates on the basis of personal whim and caprice. But we must regard God as at least *personal* or else we are assuming that He is less than we are in stature and in spiritual possibilities. We are personal; we would not be this if the Ground of our existence were not. Nothing like personality would have evolved, were not the universe shot through with Personality from the beginning. This is simply the law of conservation, scientifically speaking. When more comes out of less, that is magic; and it is certainly not in line with our notions of scientific law to assume that human personality as an effect can be traced back ultimately to a cause which is less than personal. And even using the word "personal" we are of course anthropomorphic, but naturally we must be, in talking about anything; man's words are all that we have to describe either the contents of an atom or the meaning of the universe.

If, then, God is personal, that means He is articulate and capable of what Martin Buber calls the *I-Thou* relationship. This being one of the highest qualities of personality as we know it in ourselves, God is capable of no less than this.

That God has related Himself to us is not thus proven; but it is not implausible to expect that He has, does, and will. The experience of the people of God, of the old and new Israel, of the people of the Bible and of the Church, is that God has dealt with us, does deal with us and will continue to deal with us. This he does, of course, in manifold ways, but especially when we grow quiet, shut out the clamor of the world and the claims of the idols. Especially does He do this as we worship. Our adoration, our contrition, our prayers, and our acts of thanksgiving do not fall on deaf ears. These are not merely psychological exercises—though they are this; they are met on the other side by God's action. When we raise our hand to take God's hand, He does take our hand. The experience of relating ourselves to Him can be deeper, more beneficial to our total health, if it exceeds our conscious experience and spills over into our unconscious levels. Thus it is no substitution of psychology for real religion to give thought to the most effective ways of worship. The most effective ways of worship are those which direct our conscious thoughts and mold our unconscious impulses so that to our depths we have confidence in God's grace and are fully receptive to it.

But rationalism and individualism have a large enough place in our culture that we are apt to strike another objection at this point. Some people who might be willing to go and have their minds reasoned with by a lecture or sermon, will say, "If you say that worship, especially liturgical worship, does things automatically to my unconscious, I don't want that sort of thing done to me, by some clever process" —recoiling somewhat as one would from benefits held forth by a hypnotist. There is a good side to this type of objection. We are meant to be individuals, responsible in integrity for our own lives and decisions and we rightly fear to be influenced unconsciously by influences which are not under the control of our minds. But to the objection itself two things should be said: first, we are always being influenced in unconscious levels by forces larger than ourselves. As we have already seen, the whole milieu in which we live, the secular atmosphere of our daily lives, the means of communication and entertainment, are constantly projecting—or more strictly speaking, injecting—into our unconscious minds impressions, ideals, urges. There is no way to insulate our depths from influence. The important thing is to keep a balance in the influences brought to bear upon us. In worship we place ourselves in a specialized atmosphere in which the most wholesome things can reach us—this is the *culture within the culture* which we have been discussing.

Second, we really are in essential control of the situation if we decide with our minds what things are right and true and would be healthful if they were deeply informing our inner lives. Then we need not fear the process itself; indeed, we will welcome it. If the Christian answers to fear, guilt, inhibition, frustration, indecision, loneliness and meaninglessness are the wrong answers, then, of course, we don't want to stock our unconscious minds with the symbols of these wrong answers; but if we believe that they are the right answers, and our minds have decided that in our lives we should take the risk that they are, then we should take advantage of the means which will allow the answers to reach us more deeply, less superficially. To use a variant of an example used earlier, if a doctor convinces his patient that he needs an operation, explaining to him as best he can the whole picture, the need to be met, the means to be used, and the expected results, *and* if the patient trusts the doctor, then he will go under the anaesthetic for the operation though he is not in control of the steps being taken to effect the general end to which he has committed himself. So in the realm of the spirit. If a man recognizes his needs, if he believes that the answer of the Christian Faith will meet those needs, if he understands the meaning of what he does in participating in worship and of the symbols being used for his help, and over all if he trusts God, then he can go to Church, relax, and drink deeply of all that is meant for the nourishment of his spirit and for the development of his sensitivity to the divine Presence—all that is meant to take him beyond anxiety.

# INDEX OF SUBJECTS

(References to principal discussions are italicized)

147